Advising Families on Succession Planning:
The High Price of Not Talking

Ian M. Hull

Advising Families on Succession Planning: The High Price of Not Talking
© LexisNexis Canada Inc. 2005
September 2005

All rights reserved. No part of this publication may be reproduced, stored in any material form (including photocopying or storing it in any medium by electronic means and whether or not transiently or incidentally to some other use of this publication) without the written permission of the copyright holder except in accordance with the provisions of the Copyright Act. Applications for the copyright holder's written permission to reproduce any part of this publication should be addressed to the publisher.

Warning: The doing of an unauthorized act in relation to a copyrighted work may result in both a civil claim for damages and criminal prosecution.

Members of the LexisNexis Group worldwide

Canada	LexisNexis Canada Inc, 123 Commerce Valley Drive E., MARKHAM, Ontario
Argentina	Abeledo Perrot, Jurisprudencia Argentina and Depalma, BUENOS AIRES
Australia	Butterworths, a Division of Reed International Books Australia Pty Ltd, CHATSWOOD, New South Wales
Austria	ARD Betriebsdienst and Verlag Orac, VIENNA
Chile	Publitecsa and Conosur Ltda, SANTIAGO DE CHILE
Czech Republic	Orac sro, PRAGUE
France	Éditions du Juris-Classeur SA, PARIS
Hong Kong	Butterworths Asia (Hong Kong), HONG KONG
Hungary	Hvg Orac, BUDAPEST
India	Butterworths India, NEW DELHI
Ireland	Butterworths (Ireland) Ltd, DUBLIN
Italy	Giuffré, MILAN
Malaysia	Malayan Law Journal Sdn Bhd, KUALA LUMPUR
New Zealand	Butterworths of New Zealand, WELLINGTON
Poland	Wydawnictwa Prawnicze PWN, WARSAW
Singapore	Butterworths Asia, SINGAPORE
South Africa	Butterworth Publishers (Pty) Ltd, DURBAN
Switzerland	Stämpfli Verlag AG, BERNE
United Kingdom	Butterworths Tolley, a Division of Reed Elsevier (UK), LONDON, WC2A
USA	LexisNexis, DAYTON, Ohio

Library and Archives Canada Cataloguing in Publication

Hull, Ian M
  Advising families on succession planning : the high price of not talking / Ian M. Hull.

Includes index.
ISBN 0-433-45112-2

  1. Estate planning--Canada. I. Title.

KE5974.H84 2005   346.7105'2   C2005-905431-X
KF750.H84 2005

Printed and bound in Canada.

Reprint #6.

About the Author

Ian M. Hull is an experienced practitioner with Hull & Hull, Barristers and Solicitors, practising in the area of estates, trusts and capacity litigation. He is the author of numerous articles and texts in the Estates/Trusts/Wills area, and is a member of STEP Canada. In addition, he serves on the Editorial Advisory Board of the Canadian Estate Administration Guide, is a past member of the Executive of the Trusts and Estates Section of the Canadian Bar Association (Ontario Section) and a former trustee of the Metropolitan Toronto Lawyers Association. He is a lecturer for the Bar Admission Course for the Law Society of Upper Canada and a frequent guest lecturer for the Canadian Bar Association and the Law Society of Upper Canada. He also maintains a specialized mediation practice focusing on pre-death and post-death estate resolutions as an estate mediator at Hull Estate Mediation Inc.

TABLE OF CONTENTS

About the Author iii

CHAPTER 1: **The High Price of Not Talking** 1

Protect Your Estate with Advance Planning — And an Open Dialogue 1
The Family Conference Solution 2
About this Book 4

PART 1 — A Wills and Estates Primer

CHAPTER 2: **What an Estate Plan Should Accomplish** 7

CHAPTER 3: **What is a Will?** 9

Important Sections of a Will 9
    Property Division 9
    Executor 10
    Other Clauses 10
Dying Without a Will (Intestacy) 11
Types of Wills 11
Amending Your Will 12

CHAPTER 4: **How to Bulletproof Your Will** 13

#1 — Make Sure You Have Proof of Your Mental Capacity to
    Sign a Will 13
#2 — Protect Against Claims of Undue Influence 14
#3 — Ensure Your Will is Properly Executed 14
#4 — Properly Document any Gifts You Make During Your Lifetime 15
#5 — Carefully Consider any Unequal Treatment of Your Beneficiaries 15
#6 — Will Drafting — Lose Your Gift if You Challenge the Will 16
#7 — Contracts Not to Contest Will 16
#8 — Don't Make Casual "Will Like" Dispositions 17

CHAPTER 5: **The Role of the Executor** 19

Collecting and Distributing Assets 20
    Applying for Probate 21
    Timing of Distributions 21
Other Duties of the Executor 22
    Making Funeral Arrangements 22

vi TABLE OF CONTENTS

Locating the Will...22
Filing the Final Tax Return 22
Providing Information to Beneficiaries 22
The Executor's Fees...23
Use of Professionals by the Executor..24
Removing Executors 24

CHAPTER 6:   The Executor's Income Tax and Accounting Obligations...25

Income Tax Filings 25
Accounting Obligations 26
Informal Accounts...27
Formal Accounts 27
Investment of Estate Assets 27

CHAPTER 7:   The Recreational Property Conundrum 29

Plan for Capital Gains Taxes 30

CHAPTER 8:   Taxes That Arise on Death 31

Capital Gains Taxes 31
Principal Residence Exemption..34
Tax on RRSP and RRIF Assets..34
Reducing Probate Fees...34
Other Tax-Reduction Strategies 35

CHAPTER 9:   Trusts 37

Advantages of a Trust 38
Choosing Your Trustee 39
Incentive Trusts..41

CHAPTER 10:   Estate Freezes 43

Use of Family Trusts..45

CHAPTER 11:   Power of Attorney 47

Power of Attorney for Property...47
Mental Capacity Required..48
Restrictions...48
Choice of Attorney 49
Challenges to a Power of Attorney for Property 51
Power of Attorney for Personal Care 52

PART 2 — Why Estate Plans are Challenged — And What it Costs

CHAPTER 12: Ten Most Frequent Causes of Estate Litigation ... 55

Ten Most Frequent Causes 55
Claims Against the Will 58
Dependants' Relief Claims 59
    Family Law Entitlements 60
    Breach of Contract 61
    Constructive Trust 61

CHAPTER 13: The Legal Process and its Costs 63

What Are Legal Costs? 63
Stages in a Court Action 64
    Stage 1 — Order Organizing the Litigation 64
    Stage 2 — Collecting and Disclosing Evidence 64
    Stage 3 — Discoveries 65
    Stage 4 — Pre-trial Conference 65
    Stage 5 — Trial 65
    Stage 6 — Appeal 66
Mediation 66

PART 3 — The Family Conference Solution

CHAPTER 14: Family Constitutions 71

Introductory Wording 71
Wording of Family Constitution 72

CHAPTER 15: Before the Conference 75

Who to Invite 75
Minor Children 76
Preparing the Agenda 77
Family Conference Agenda 77
Choice of Chairperson 81

CHAPTER 16: At the Conference 83

Role of the Mediator 83
Family Conference Agreement 84
    Family Conference Agreement of the Gordon Family 84
Rules for the Meeting 85
    Rules for the Gordon Family Conference 86

Need for Full Disclosure 87
Course of the Conference 90

CHAPTER 17: If Family Members Will Not Approve Your Plan.....93

If Family Members Will Not Attend the Family Conference 93
If Family Members Object to Your Proposed Estate Plan 94

CHAPTER 18: Steps to Take After the Conference 97

Implementing Your Estate Plan 97
Review Your Estate Plan Regularly 98

CHAPTER 19: Conclusion 99

Index 101

CHAPTER 1

THE HIGH PRICE OF NOT TALKING

As an estate litigator, I am paid to be a fighter, and when I chose this profession, I knew that managing conflict would be part of my life. But all of the legal training in the world could not prepare me for the horrors that I have seen family members inflict on one another when battling over an estate. Children suing mothers, siblings bitterly torn apart, elderly parents shamelessly manipulated for gain, and millions of dollars wasted fighting over assets that diminish with each pre-trial motion and new claim. The really sad part is that, in the majority of cases, these horrors are entirely preventable.

The costs of litigation are enormous — both financially and emotionally. The value of your estate can be significantly eroded, which means less of your money will go to the beneficiaries you have chosen. And your family may be permanently torn apart and relationships ruined as a result of the litigation.

PROTECT YOUR ESTATE WITH ADVANCE PLANNING — AND AN OPEN DIALOGUE

The good news is that most estate litigation can be avoided with advance planning. You can significantly reduce the likelihood of having your will challenged by taking two preliminary steps:

- Develop an effective and comprehensive estate plan that directs who is to receive your assets on your death
- Consult with your intended beneficiaries in advance so that they understand the reasoning behind your estate planning decisions and accept those decisions as fair.

It is important that you take both steps. Traditional estate planning is focused on developing a comprehensive estate plan that includes the writing of a will and strategies to minimize your estate's tax liability. This is still important, as there is simply no substitute for the skill and advice that your financial and legal advisors can bring to the estate planning process.

But developing an estate plan is only one part of protecting your estate from litigation. If you want to minimize the likelihood of your will being contested, you need to consult your family members about your intentions, and if necessary, work with them to obtain their agreement.

This requires a shift in how we think about estate planning. A successful estate plan is no longer solely developed from the top down; it also involves planning from the bottom up. In my experience, family members are far less likely to challenge a will if they have been given an explanation of the reasons for the distribution of property and have had an opportunity to express their opinions about that distribution. And the best way to ensure that your family members are in agreement with your plan is to hold a professionally-mediated family conference.

THE FAMILY CONFERENCE SOLUTION

At a family conference, you will have an opportunity to explain your wishes to family members and describe how you intend to dispose of your estate. You will also be able to assess their reactions and determine if changes to the plan are necessary.

For example, you may intend to leave the family cottage to both your children, but at the family conference you may discover that one child would instead actually prefer to receive cash. Conversely, you may find that there are assets that you intended to leave to one child that both your children want. A family conference can provide a forum for discussion that ensures both you and your intended beneficiaries are comfortable with the end result.

A family conference also allows you to address the emotional issues that arise around a will. The reaction of beneficiaries to a proposed estate plan is often coloured by their personal feelings, particularly if they will receive less than they expect. In many cases, if they are advised of the real reasons underlying the decisions about how the assets are to be distributed, they will be able to live with the estate plan. No one wants to leave a legacy of ill-will and acrimony between their children, and the family conference process is an excellent way to minimize the risk of this occurring.

Best Estate Intentions Can be Misunderstood

Catherine Randall is an 80-year-old widow who owns her own home in a good neighbourhood and has savings of about $250,000. Mrs. Randall has two children, Michael and Elizabeth, both in their forties. Michael is a happily married and successful businessman who earns a six-figure salary. He has a large home and cottage and three children who all attend private school. Mrs. Randall is, understandably, very proud of her son.

Elizabeth has been less successful financially than her brother. She has tried many careers but never stayed with one for long. Elizabeth lives in a rental apartment and is often short of cash, particularly during the frequent periods when she is between jobs. Mrs. Randall often steps in to help pay her bills during those times. In order to ensure Elizabeth's long-term financial security, Mrs. Randall intends to leave her home and most of her savings to Elizabeth on her death.

Mrs. Randall did not intend to tell Michael of her plans before her death. She believed that he would know that her decision to leave the bulk of her estate to his sister was because she respected his ability to support himself, and reflected her pride in him. She was shocked when her financial advisor suggested that Michael might see her estate plan as the exact opposite, and think that she had disinherited him because she was disappointed in him for unknown reasons. Mrs. Randall's advisor also cautioned her that since her children would learn of her wishes at the same time they were coping with her loss, their emotional reactions might be exacerbated.

Mrs. Randall's financial advisor recommended that she hold a professionally-mediated family conference to explain the reasons for her estate plan to both children. Although Michael was initially surprised by her proposed plan, after some thought he agreed that it was fair.

Michael told his mother that there were two gifts he would like from her estate: his father's stamp collection, which had strong emotional significance to him, and some funds to help pay for his children's upcoming university education. His mother had been unaware of his desire for the stamp collection, and intended to sell it and add the proceeds of the sale to her estate. When she learned of his wishes, she arranged to leave the collection to him. She also set up a trust fund with $50,000 of her savings for the university education costs of her three grandchildren.

In the end, both Mrs. Randall and her children were pleased with the results of the meeting. Mrs. Randall was particularly pleased that her decision to leave the bulk of her estate to Elizabeth did not seem to be causing animosity between the children. Michael was relieved that his

> mother's decisions meant that he would not be expected to support his sister financially after his mother was gone, and he was pleased that his mother had recognized his children. Elizabeth was, naturally, happy to have her long-term financial worries alleviated.

ABOUT THIS BOOK

I have written this book to help you avoid the disasters that I have seen other families face. It is divided into three Parts.

- Part 1 — A will and estates primer, takes you through the steps in the estate planning process and discusses the most common mistakes people make and how they can be prevented.
- Part 2 — Why estate plans are challenged and what it costs, describes the circumstances in which estate plans are challenged, and why contesting a will can be so costly and time-consuming for everyone involved.
- Part 3 — The family conference solution, highlights the importance of considering the wishes of your beneficiaries, and takes you through the family conference process step-by-step.

If you are reluctant to hold a family conference, consider the fact that if your beneficiaries think your estate plan is unfair, they may challenge it after you are gone. This could result in your wishes being ignored, your hard-earned money being spent on lawyers and accountants, and your family being torn apart — a high price to pay for not talking.

PART 1

A WILLS AND ESTATES PRIMER

Chapter 2

What an Estate Plan Should Accomplish

Before embarking on the professionally-mediated family conference process, you will need a basic understanding of what estate planning is meant to accomplish.

Ideally, your estate plan should:

- **Ensure your assets go to the people you intend**. A will is an essential part of every estate plan, because without it your assets will be distributed in accordance with provincial law — which may not be to the beneficiaries you intended. In addition, if you die without a will, provincial law will direct who will administer your estate, and again, it may not be the person you would have chosen.
- **Reduce your estate's tax bill**. Your estate may be liable for a substantial tax bill on your death. That is because you are deemed to dispose of all your capital property when you die, and your estate must pay any applicable capital gains tax. In addition, assets you hold in registered plans (like RRSPs and RRIFs) lose their tax-sheltered status when you die, unless you name your spouse as beneficiary. You may also have to pay probate fees to confirm the validity of your will. Advance planning will allow you to substantially reduce the taxes and probate fees that you have to pay.
- **Protect your assets if you become disabled**. In addition to dealing with your assets at death, an estate plan can also address what happens to your assets if you become physically or mentally disabled during your lifetime and can no longer look after your own affairs. A power of attorney lets you choose a trusted friend, family member or advisor to manage your affairs if you are unable to do so.

This Part of the book will look at each of the three components to an estate plan — wills, tax reduction strategies, and powers of attorney — and the steps you can take to protect them from challenge.

CHAPTER 3

WHAT IS A WILL?

A will is a written statement that sets out how you want your assets to be disposed of on your death. A will creates an *almost* unchangeable estate plan that can only be varied if everyone with a financial interest in the estate agrees, so it is important that it accurately describes your wishes. After you die, your will provides the framework for the appointment of the executor who is responsible for the administration of your estate. Your will gives the executor the power to deal with your assets and to distribute them to the beneficiaries you have selected. Your will may also be subject to various claims by unhappy beneficiaries. These claims are discussed in Chapter 12.

IMPORTANT SECTIONS OF A WILL

The two most important sections in your will are the provisions which dispose of your property and the provisions which appoint an executor.

Property Division

Your will specifies how you want your assets distributed. You can distribute your estate by specific bequests, by income gifts and by a share in the residue. A specific bequest includes a gift of a sum of money or a specific asset. For example, "I give the Canadian Cancer Society the sum of $50,000" or "I give my daughter Harriet Jones my pearl necklace and my diamond engagement ring." Gifts can also be made to more than one person. For example, you can leave your cottage jointly to your three children in your will.

You can also give people a right to use an asset during their lifetime, but not the right to dispose of it on their death. For example, you can specify in your will that you want your second husband to have the right to use your cottage while he is alive, but that it is to your children by your first marriage on his death.

Your will can also provide for a gift of income (but not the asset itself) by creating a trust in your will. The executor invests the trust funds and your beneficiary receives the income. The amount of income the beneficiary receives will depend on the success of the executor's investment strategies. We will discuss the use of trusts in more detail in Chapter 7.

Once the specific bequests are made, any trusts are created, and all taxes and debts are paid, the remainder of the estate is known as the residue. Your will must specify how the residue is to be divided. For example, you could state "I leave my husband Thomas Wilson the residue of my estate". The residue can also be divided into equal or non-equal shares (for example, one person could receive 20 per cent of the residue and another person could receive the remaining 80 per cent).

Most estate litigation arises over how the assets are divided. In order to ensure that the assets are distributed the way that you want and that funds are properly paid out by the estate, you should have a lawyer prepare your will rather than preparing it yourself or using a wills kit.

Executor

The executor is the person who manages your estate. You may also want to appoint an alternate executor in case the first executor is unable or unwilling to act. The job of an executor is complex, demanding and time-consuming. Executors are entitled to be paid for their services, and their fees are a common source of litigation. We will look at the executor's duties and how to reduce the likelihood of litigation over their fees in Chapter 5.

Other Clauses

There are a number of other clauses that may be included in your will. For example, if you are leaving assets to minor children, your will must contain a clause appointing a trustee to manage the property for them until they reach the age of majority. If you have minor children, you may want to appoint a guardian for them in your will. You may also want to detail your funeral arrangements. Your lawyer will discuss your personal circumstances with you to determine which clauses are appropriate for your will.

DYING WITHOUT A WILL (INTESTACY)

Dying without a will is far more common than you might expect. Over one-third of adult Canadians do not have a will. This is because people are naturally reluctant to talk about, or prepare for, their own deaths. However, if you do not prepare a will, you give up the right to direct how your property will be divided and who will administer your estate.

If you die without a will (intestate), provincial intestacy laws govern how your assets will be distributed. In most cases, this will not be the way you had intended. While many people think that their spouse will automatically inherit all of their assets if they die without a will, that is not the case. In most provinces, while your spouse will receive a preferential share of your estate, the balance of your estate is divided equally between your spouse and your children.

> **Do You Know How Your Province Will Divide Your Estate?**
>
> In Ontario, if you die without a will and have a spouse and two children, your spouse will receive the first $200,000 of your estate plus one-third of any value of the estate over $200,000, while your two children will each receive an equal share of the remaining two-thirds of the estate. If your estate is worth $800,000, your spouse will receive $400,000 and each child will receive $200,000.

If you have minor children, it is essential that you have a will. If you die intestate and your children are under 18 years of age, the court, and not your spouse or a person you would have selected, will manage their share of your estate until they turn 18. Furthermore, once your children turn 18, they have the right to have the money paid to them — which means you cannot delay the distribution of their share of your estate until they are older and more responsible, something many parents do in their wills.

Dying intestate also means you are unable to choose the person who will administer your estate. Instead, the court will appoint an administrator, and again, it may not be the person you would have selected.

TYPES OF WILLS

There are two types of wills — handwritten and typewritten. Both types of will are legal.

A handwritten will is called a "holograph will". In order to be valid, it must be *entirely* in your own handwriting and be signed by you and dated. No witnesses are necessary.

A typewritten or "formal" will is usually prepared by a lawyer. It must be signed by you and witnessed by two individuals who are present at the same time, and who are not beneficiaries or spouses of beneficiaries under the will. If a typewritten will is not properly witnessed, it is invalid and intestacy laws will apply unless you have an earlier, valid will.

Although do-it-yourself or preprinted will kits are widely available, I do not recommend their use. There are few legal minefields greater than drafting a will, and I regularly address disputes over do-it-yourself wills that could have been prevented if a lawyer had been initially consulted.

AMENDING YOUR WILL

Once you have prepared your will, you must review it regularly to ensure that it is kept up-to-date. If any of the following events occur, you may need to either amend your will or prepare a new one:

- You divorce or remarry.
- You live with a common-law or same-sex spouse for more than three years.
- You move to another province or country.
- A child or grandchild is born.
- A beneficiary or your proposed executor predeceases you.
- Your financial circumstances change.

Even if none of those events occur, you should still review your will every few years to make sure it still reflects your intentions.

CHAPTER 4

HOW TO BULLETPROOF YOUR WILL

There are a number of steps you can take when preparing your will to reduce the likelihood of it being successfully challenged. In particular, your will needs to comply with all relevant laws. This means ensuring that, when you prepared the will, you had the necessary mental capacity to sign it, you were not unduly influenced by anyone while it was being prepared, and that the will was properly executed.

If your will is successfully challenged and you have a valid prior will, your earlier will takes effect. If you do not have a valid prior will, the intestacy rules in your province apply.

If you want to bulletproof your will, here are some steps you should take:

#1 — MAKE SURE YOU HAVE PROOF OF YOUR MENTAL CAPACITY TO SIGN A WILL

A will is invalid if you did not have the mental capacity to sign it when the will was made. A beneficiary who is unhappy with the will (or someone who has been left out entirely) may attack the will on the basis that you did not know and understand the nature and effect of the terms in your will. A court will then enquire as to whether you understood who would benefit under your estate at the time you signed the will.

If you have any concerns that your will may be challenged on this basis, make sure your lawyer takes detailed notes about your instructions and your ability to make and understand those instructions. You should also ask your doctor to prepare detailed notes on your mental capacity. Because your doctor's evidence on the issue of your mental capacity may carry more weight than the evidence of your lawyer, make sure the doctor is advised that he or she is to specifically assess your mental capacity. If your will is challenged, the beneficiaries to whom you have left your assets have the onus of proving that you had the necessary mental capacity to make the will. The notes of your lawyer and doctor, made at the time you signed the will, will be very useful to them.

You should avoid preparing a will during a temporary period of physical or mental frailty or illness. If at all possible, it is better to wait until you have recovered from the illness before preparing a new will as this will reduce the likelihood of a successful challenge.

#2 — PROTECT AGAINST CLAIMS OF UNDUE INFLUENCE

Your will can also be challenged on the basis that someone has forced you to sign a document that does not reflect your real intentions. For example, if an elderly widower leaves all of his estate to his housekeeper and nothing to his children, the children may claim that the housekeeper coerced him into leaving everything to her.

If this type of claim is made, the court will consider the personal circumstances surrounding the will. For the claim to succeed, evidence of real coercion must be provided. In general, if the person making the will (the testator) is elderly, unhealthy, frail or highly dependent on one individual, the court will closely examine the testator's mental capabilities when the will was signed to determine whether he or she was coerced into doing so. If any of those circumstances apply to you when you are making your will, have both your lawyer and your doctor prepare detailed notes on your mental condition that can be used later if your will is challenged.

#3 — ENSURE YOUR WILL IS PROPERLY EXECUTED

Your will can also be challenged if it is not properly executed. Your lawyer will ensure that it is properly witnessed and that the witnesses sign the necessary affidavits.

If you make subsequent changes to your will, they must also be properly signed and witnessed. If, for example, you decide to change a gift you have made by crossing out that section of the will, you may invalidate the whole will. To make a change, your lawyer will either prepare an addition to the will (called a "codicil"), or simply prepare a new will.

#4 — PROPERLY DOCUMENT ANY GIFTS YOU MAKE DURING YOUR LIFETIME

If you are making large gifts during your lifetime, make sure they are properly documented in case they are later challenged. This is particularly important if you are making unequal gifts — for example, if you give money to only one of your children. This is true even if you have a good reason for making unequal gifts, such as when one child has been your primary caregiver and you want to ensure that he or she is financially compensated.

Your other children may not be aware of the gifts until you die, and they may object at that time. As with a challenge to a will, they can claim you did not have the mental capacity to make the gifts, or that you were unduly influenced. If you consult with your lawyer at the time you make the gifts, your lawyer can prepare appropriate legal documents such as deeds and trusts. Your lawyer, with the help of your doctor, can also document your mental capacity to make the gifts.

#5 — CAREFULLY CONSIDER ANY UNEQUAL TREATMENT OF YOUR BENEFICIARIES

While you may have good reasons for treating your children unequally, such gifts can cause enormous friction within a family. For example, unequal gifts may occur when one child has looked after their aging parents and has made personal and financial sacrifices to do so. Those parents often want to show their financial gratitude to that child in their will. However, the other children often perceive this as a suggestion that they were not loved as much as the caregiver child.

Even a modest unequal treatment can cause this reaction. For example, giving one child who was your caregiver a gift of a $25,000 Guaranteed Investment Certificate (GIC) that is not given to the other children may cause serious conflict within your family. If that child had a power of attorney over your property and the other children are sufficiently dissatisfied, they may question all of the financial conduct of the caregiver child and request a full audit of his or her financial activities on your behalf — something that is both expensive and time-consuming.

If you are going to make unequal gifts, you should fully disclose the gift, and your reasons for it, to your other children. As we will discuss later in this book, a family conference provides an excellent opportunity to explain your decision to your whole family — and potentially save your estate the costs of a legal battle.

#6 — WILL DRAFTING — LOSE YOUR GIFT IF YOU CHALLENGE THE WILL

You can effectively persuade your beneficiaries to not frivolously contest your will by including a clause in the will that provides that if a person who is entitled to receive a gift under your will challenges the will, they will lose that gift. These clauses are known as *in terrorem* (which appropriately means "in fear" in Latin) clauses. While courts will closely scrutinize an *in terrorem* clause before enforcing it, this type of clause can be an effective tool in protecting your will from challenge.

These clauses are particularly effective if you are giving your children unequal shares of your estate. If the gift to one child is substantial, even if it is less than that of your other children, that child may be dissuaded from challenging the will. *In terrorem* clauses will not be effective, however, if the person challenging the will has received nothing under the will, or if the gift is so modest that he or she is prepared to risk losing it.

#7 — CONTRACTS NOT TO CONTEST WILL

Situations occasionally arise where the expected beneficiaries jointly agree in advance not to contest the will as long as it divides the assets evenly between them. For example, if a parent has periodically shifted their favour from one child to another, and has periodically changed their will to give a greater amount to the child then in favour, the children may jointly enter into an agreement to divide the assets equally on death, regardless of the terms of the will. They may also agree that any gifts made within the six months prior to death should be redistributed equally among the children.

A family conference is an excellent way to address this situation. It allows the children to tell the parent that they want to share equally in the estate, and that none of them, even the child then in favour, want an unequal distribution of assets.

#8 — DON'T MAKE CASUAL "WILL LIKE" DISPOSITIONS

Once you have made a valid will, be careful not to make "will like" dispositions in any of your letters or other correspondence that are inconsistent with the terms of the will. These may be treated as revoking the terms of the will and creating a new one, even if that is not your intention.

> **When is a Letter More Than a Letter?**
>
> Jane Armbruster was a retired nurse with no children, and was a devoted aunt to her nieces and nephews. She had a formal will dividing all of her $1 million estate equally between them. She regularly wrote letters to all of her family members, and since she was not comfortable using a computer, they were all in her own handwriting.
>
> After she died, her will was located, as was a letter she later wrote to one nephew that said that she was "very pleased with the work done by the Feed the Hungry Food Bank" and that she expected "they should receive something from my estate". She also wrote that "this letter should help and assist you with the division of my estate". Because the letter was dated, in Jane's own handwriting, and used will-like language, the Feed the Hungry Food Bank took the position that it was a valid holograph will, and that it should revoke the earlier formal will in favour of the nieces and nephews.
>
> The family believed that the letter was simply a handwritten note with no legal effect and that the formal will should prevail. They were surprised to learn that a court would likely decide the situation had arisen because of their aunt's mistake, and that her estate would bear the costs of the litigation, which could be substantial.
>
> They were also surprised to learn that the Feed the Hungry Food Bank, like many charities, was not prepared to simply defer to the family, and intended to proceed with their claim against Mrs. Armbruster's estate, even though their success would mean that the family would receive nothing from the estate. In the end, the Feed the Hungry Food Bank and the nieces and nephews settled the claim in order to avoid the costs of litigation.

All of these steps are either essential, or useful, in protecting your will from being successfully challenged. However, because estate litigation is so costly, you also want to protect against unsuccessful challenges to your will. Even if the will is ultimately upheld, the estate will have spent thousands of dollars on legal fees — so even if you win, you lose. The best way to successfully protect your will from challenge is to ensure that your beneficiaries are satisfied with your disposition of assets.

Chapter 5

The Role of the Executor

Choosing an executor is one of the most important decisions you will make when preparing your will. Many people consider it an honour to be named as executor, in the same way that it is an honour to be chosen as a godparent. However, the role of executor goes far beyond an honorary role.

It is important to consider your choice of executor very carefully. You must select someone that you trust absolutely, since they will be managing your financial affairs. The person selected must also be capable of acting impartially on behalf of your estate, regardless of their personal feelings about your estate and or your beneficiaries.

The executor's job is also challenging and time-consuming. You should make sure the person you select is willing to assume the responsibility. An executor is personally liable for mistakes made paying out the estate, so he or she cannot take the job lightly. While it is impossible to guarantee that someone who has consented to act as your executor will still be willing to do so at the time of your death, you should ensure that at the time you prepare your will, your selected executor is willing to serve in that role.

Ideally, your executor should have good business sense and know how to manage financial assets. He or she does not need to be an accountant or lawyer or investment advisor, but does need to be able to hire the necessary expertise that your estate may require. For example, your executor does not need to know all the intricate tax rules that apply on death, but does need to obtain professional tax advice to ensure that the tax rules are fully reviewed before your estate is paid out.

Your executor should also live near where the estate will be administered so he or she can cope with the practical details of managing your estate, such as dealing with financial institutions and possible court applications. If your proposed executor lives 3,000 kilometres away, it will be difficult for him or her to handle the day-to-day management required.

Your executor should also be young and healthy enough that he or she is not likely to predecease you. If you name someone as an executor who dies before you, you will need to amend your will to provide a new executor (unless you have already named an alternate executor).

COLLECTING AND DISTRIBUTING ASSETS

The executor is responsible for administering and distributing your estate as set out in your will. The will itself provides the executor with the authority to act and allows him or her to deal with the assets immediately upon death.

The executor is responsible for collecting all of the assets of the estate and selling those assets not specifically disposed of in the will. He or she then pays any debts of the estate, including all outstanding bills, funeral expenses and any amounts owing to the Canada Revenue Agency.

The executor must also ensure that there are no outstanding or potential claims against the estate. There are a variety of different claims that can be made against the estate, including claims by a spouse who is unhappy with the will. We will discuss these claims in detail in Chapter 12.

Once the debts have been paid and all claims resolved, the executor will distribute the assets as set out in the will to the beneficiaries named therein.

Surprisingly, the distribution of the personal property and personal effects is a significant source of estate litigation. Beneficiaries often feel entitled to specific assets they believe were promised to them, even if those instructions are not contained in the will. A family conference at which you tell your beneficiaries what you are leaving them will prevent this type of disappointment. You can help your executor by setting out the distribution of valuable personal effects in your will. However, you will need to amend your will if you change your intentions, or if you dispose of the items during your lifetime.

Less valuable items can still be very contentious. You can help your executor dispose of them by providing handwritten summaries of those items and their intended recipients. Family members generally respect these summaries and they help reduce conflict. At your family conference, consider asking all of your beneficiaries which of your less valuable items they want.

> **Small Items — Huge Rifts**
>
> As a child, Mary Hopkinson was responsible for polishing her mother's brass candlesticks every weekend. Her mother always told her that when she died, Mary would receive the candlesticks. Mary was in her forties when her mother died. There was no mention of the brass candlesticks, which were not valuable, in her mother's will. When Mary asked for them she was told that a niece who had always liked them had taken them and was unwilling to return them. Thirty years later, Mary was still furious with her niece over an inexpensive pair of brass candlesticks.

Applying for Probate

The executor needs to decide whether or not to apply to the courts for letters probate. Letters probate confirm that the will is valid and that the executor has the authority to act. Because most provinces charge a fee (which can be more than 1 per cent of the value of estate assets in some provinces) for issuing letters probate, an executor should apply for letter probate only if it is absolutely necessary.

The executor should first contact the deceased's financial institution to determine if it will require letters probate before releasing the estate's assets. If the amount involved is small, financial institutions will generally only require a notarial copy of the will to release them. However, each bank, and sometimes each branch, has its own rules, which may also depend on whether the branch manager was familiar with the deceased. You will also often require letters probate to transfer ownership of real property.

Timing of Distributions

Beneficiaries often believe that the executor is taking too long to distribute the estate. There is a general rule that an executor has one year from the date of death to distribute the property of the deceased. However, not all estates are immediately distributable. Sometimes the will creates trusts in which assets are held, or there are circumstances in which it is not financially prudent to immediately distribute certain assets (such as when a term deposit would have to be redeemed early at a penalty).

The distribution of the estate may also be delayed if the executor is required to investigate and possibly defend the estate against potential claims. He or she needs to explain to the beneficiaries the anticipated timing of the distribution of the estate, so they do not expect an unrealistically early distribution.

You also need to give your executor sufficient powers and flexibility to properly manage your assets during the period before the estate is distributed. For example, your executor should be given the authority to change the estate's investment strategy to respond to changes in the economy or in the stock market so as to maximize the return to the beneficiaries.

OTHER DUTIES OF THE EXECUTOR

In addition to collecting and distributing assets, executors also have several other duties to perform in the course of settling an estate.

Making Funeral Arrangements

One of the executor's first duties is to arrange the funeral. If you have specific instructions as to how you want your funeral to be conducted, you should let your executor know or include these instructions in your will.

Locating the Will

The executor needs to ensure that he or she is acting under the authority of the deceased's most current will. The executor should search the deceased's home and papers to determine whether the will under which he or she is acting has been amended or revoked.

Filing the Final Tax Return

The executor is also responsible for filing a final tax return for both the deceased and the estate and ensuring that any outstanding income tax is paid. We will discuss the executor's filing and accounting obligations in detail in Chapter 6.

Providing Information to Beneficiaries

The executor is also responsible for providing information about the estate to the beneficiaries. Beneficiaries who are not kept informed about an estate's accounts often become frustrated with the executor and are more likely to consider litigation. However, once a beneficiary has been paid his or her bequest, that beneficiary is no longer entitled to information about the estate's assets.

THE EXECUTOR'S FEES

An executor is entitled to a fee for his or her services. Although courts have established general guidelines for appropriate fees, the actual amount of the fee is frequently the basis of litigation. Dissatisfied beneficiaries often claim that the executor's fees are unduly high and seek to have them reduced.

Courts generally accept that the executor is entitled to a 2.5 per cent fee on money that comes into the estate and a 2.5 per cent fee on money paid out of the estate. In certain circumstances, an additional management fee is allowed. For example, if the executor manages a sum of money over a period of years, a management fee of two-fifths of 1 per cent of the assets is usually allowed per year. In addition, if the executor has to perform special duties on behalf of the estate, such as defending a long and bitter lawsuit, he or she may be allowed to claim a special fee.

Family members will often argue that the executor's fees should be reduced. They may claim that the estate is overly simple, and that a reduced percentage is appropriate. Or if they are dissatisfied with the executor's conduct during the estate administration (for example, the executor has not disclosed the nature and extent of the estate assets in a timely way) they may seek to reduce the compensation paid to the executor. In addition, if the beneficiaries think the executor has badly managed the estate's investments, they may request that the fees be reduced.

In determining an appropriate fee, the courts will consider the complexity of the estate. For example, a small estate with many stock holdings may be far more complicated to administer than a large estate that consists of an expensive home and one large GIC. In determining an appropriate fee, the courts will consider the complexity of the estate, the amount of time the executor spent administering the estate, the skill and ability displayed by the executor and the degree of success achieved by the executor.

If you appoint a family member as your executor, your other family members may object to fees being charged. You should have a discussion with the other family members so that they understand the usual range of executors' fees, and are aware that there could be additional special fees if the estate becomes unduly complicated.

Your will can also specify, or limit, the amount of the fees to be paid to the executor. While this can serve as a good guideline for both the executor and the beneficiaries, be careful not to set the fees too low or the executor may renounce the role. Keep in mind that the role of executor can be tremendously difficult and the fees are almost always well earned. If you restrict the fees too severely, you could lose your first choice of executor.

USE OF PROFESSIONALS BY THE EXECUTOR

The executor is responsible for determining which professionals to hire on behalf of the estate and what fees they should be paid. However, the beneficiaries will often object if professional fees substantially reduce their shares of the estate. Although the beneficiaries will criticize the executor if professional fees are too high, in many cases the executor is equally surprised by the amount charged.

You can help protect your executor from this criticism by educating the beneficiaries, and the executor, about the range of fees that professionals may charge for their work in administering the estate. You can also help reduce professional fees by ensuring that all your tax returns are properly filed during your lifetime and that all assets, including those that are offshore, are properly recorded, so that your executor does not have to clean up your estate before distributing it.

REMOVING EXECUTORS

The most vicious and personal disagreements in estate litigation often revolve around the removal of an executor. Courts are very reluctant to remove an executor, and will only do so if the executor has committed serious misconduct. However, there are numerous grounds on which misconduct can be alleged, which can lead to costly legal battles.

When you are choosing an executor, consider how likely your family members are to object to your choice. This is an important issue to be addressed at the family conference, particularly if you intend to choose a family member as executor. If it appears that your choice will create problems within your family, give instead serious consideration to appointing a professional or a trust company.

CHAPTER 6

THE EXECUTOR'S INCOME TAX AND ACCOUNTING OBLIGATIONS

The executor is responsible for the estate's income tax filings and for keeping proper records of all of the estate's financial transactions. These records are to be made available to the beneficiaries, so it is essential that they be properly prepared and maintained.

INCOME TAX FILINGS

The executor is responsible for filing the necessary tax returns with the Canada Revenue Agency. These returns can be complicated and the executor may hire an accountant to help with their preparation. The accountant's fees will be paid out of the estate's assets.

The executor is required to file the following tax returns:

- **Any previously unfiled returns.** The executor is required to file any income tax returns which the deceased failed to file in the years before his or her death. These must be filed within six months of the date of death.
- ***T1 Terminal Return.*** This return covers the period from January 1 in the year of death to the date of death. The executor must file it by the later of six months from the date of death or April 30 of the following year and pay any taxes owed at the date of death.
- ***T3 Estate Return.*** This return covers the income of the estate from the date of death to the end of the calendar year or the estate year, which is one year from the date of death. The executor chooses the time period for the return and must file the return within 90 days of the end of such year. If the estate generates income or capital gains during this period, the executor will have to pay additional taxes on behalf of the estate.

- ***T-3 Final Distribution Return.*** This return covers the income of the estate in the final year of distribution to the beneficiaries from the start of the estate year to the date of final distribution. The executor must file this return within 90 days of the year end of the estate. If the estate is distributed within the first year, this can be filed with the T1 Terminal Return.

When the executor has completed the necessary tax filings, he or she should apply for a Clearance Certificate from the Canada Revenue Agency confirming that there are no further filings or taxes owing. Once the Clearance Certificate is issued, in the absence of fraud, the executor is protected from any future income tax liability of the estate. The executor should also pay any outstanding GST owed by the estate and obtain a Clearance Certificate from Customs and Excise Canada.

ACCOUNTING OBLIGATIONS

An executor is required to keep proper records of all of the money paid out or received by the estate. The estate's accounts and records must be kept separate from the executor's personal accounts and records to minimize confusion. The executor can only avoid the obligation to make a financial accounting of the estate if all of the beneficiaries are over 18 years old and they all agree as to how the funds are distributed.

The estate's accounts are available to the beneficiaries when they request them and the executor should provide them with all the essential financial information about the estate. The accounts should be easy to understand and avoid technical accounting terms like "debit" or "credit". The executor should ensure that the beneficiaries know they have the right to a full and complete accounting of the estate's assets.

The executor usually prepares accounts every two to three years. Once either the beneficiaries or the court has approved the accounts, the executor's obligations for that accounting period are over.

There are two types of accounts: informal and formal. Informal accounts are usually sufficient, but a beneficiary may require the executor to prepare formal accounts that are submitted to a court for review.

Informal Accounts

An executor is required to keep a documentary record of all estate financial transactions, including all bank statements, invoices, cancelled cheques, brokerage statements and other documents issued by financial institutions. The executor must keep these records as it may be extremely difficult to obtain copies of them from the financial institution if questions arise years after the date of death. An executor should keep his or her own record book that sets out all expenses or bills paid by the estate, including the date, the payee, the amount paid and the reason for payment.

Formal Accounts

A beneficiary of the estate can require the executor to submit formal accounts to the court. A formal account is essentially an audit of all of the financial transactions that the executor has undertaken over the years. A formal account follows the assets from the date of death and cross-references them against all the money received and money paid out by the estate. A formal account also includes a full statement of the investments made by the executor.

If the estate's accounts become very contentious and a court audit is required, a professional will need to prepare properly formatted accounts. The professional will need all of the executor's records to prepare these accounts.

INVESTMENT OF ESTATE ASSETS

An executor should retain a qualified financial advisor to assist in investing the estate's assets. The investment advisor should document any investment plan that is prepared for the estate. This will help protect the executor from liability if the estate loses money on its investments.

CHAPTER 7

THE RECREATIONAL PROPERTY CONUNDRUM

One of the most difficult assets to deal with in an estate plan is recreational property. Whether it is a cottage, ski chalet, or some other family retreat, recreational property often plays an important role in the lives of children and other family members who have enjoyed it — and yet it creates such acrimony when the time comes for the parents to pass it on.

While it is possible to leave the property jointly to all of your children, the reality of shared ownership may be problematic. Unless your children have an extremely close relationship, they may find it difficult to make decisions about how to share the use of the property and the costs of repairs and upkeep.

> **Cottage Squabbles**
>
> After the death of their parents, brothers Tim and Peter Morden were left their family cottage in Georgian Bay where they had spent much of their childhood. Tim was a teacher with three young daughters and Peter had a demanding job as an accountant, with a spouse who worked equally hard.
>
> On July 1, Tim and his family moved to the cottage for the summer. Over the summer, he invited other friends and their children up for visits that lasted several days. When Peter and his wife arrived for their much-anticipated two-week vacation, all the bedrooms were taken and they were forced to sleep in tents. Although they liked their nieces, they did not want to spend their entire vacation with small children, or with Tim's friends. In addition, Peter enjoyed working on the property, and was frustrated that neither Tim nor his guests were willing to help him with the necessary repairs.
>
> At the end of the first year of shared ownership, Peter swore he would never return to the cottage again if his brother was there. Peter suggested that the following year Tim could have the cottage for July

and Peter could have it for August. Tim refused, saying that he had the whole summer off and he had no intention of spending that time in the city when he could be enjoying the cottage with his family. The cottage, which had been the source of many happy memories for both brothers, was now poisoning the relationship between them.

In order to avoid these types of problems, many owners choose to sell their property before death. This lets them pay the taxes that arise on the sale and include the net proceeds in the value of their estate. If their children want, they can use these proceeds to buy their own properties, with none of the problems that will arise from sharing with their siblings.

However, because of the strong emotional connection people have with their property, owners are often reluctant to sell and are determined to keep it in the family. In that case, parents should have a frank discussion with their children to determine if they really want the property. Parents sometimes find that although their adult children enjoy having a place to visit, they are unwilling to assume the responsibilities of ownership. In other cases, the children may prefer to be left other, more liquid, assets that are more useful to them at that stage of their lives. When you are aware of your children's wishes, you can make the decision as to whether it is appropriate to sell the property or leave it to one of your children.

PLAN FOR CAPITAL GAINS TAXES

If you decide to transfer recreational property to your children, you need to consider the most tax-effective way to do so. On your death, capital gains taxes will arise on the increase in value of the property (unless it is your principal residence), and those taxes could be onerous. For example, if your property has increased in value by $400,000 since you purchased it 30 years ago, about $80,000 in capital gains tax will be payable on your death. One of the best ways to cover those taxes is to use permanent life insurance. Your estate will receive the death benefit tax-free and can use the proceeds to cover the taxes that will arise.

You can also transfer all or part of the property during your lifetime to defer future capital gains. You can do this by either:

- Gifting the property to your children.
- Making one or more of the children joint owners of the property with you.

- Transferring the property to a trust, with your children named as beneficiaries.

All three transfer methods will trigger an immediate capital gain for which you are responsible. However, future capital gains will be the responsibility of your children. These will not become payable during their lifetimes so long as they continue to hold the property.

Transferring the property to a trust offers the added benefit of an independent third party (the trustee) managing the property and making maintenance and other decisions on behalf of the beneficiaries, even after your death. This can be very useful if there are otherwise irresolvable conflicts between your children, or if any of your children are unwilling to deal with all the responsibilities of ownership.

CHAPTER 8

TAXES THAT ARISE ON DEATH

Many estate plans focus on reducing the taxes payable on your death — and there is good reason for doing so. While there are no specific death or inheritance taxes in Canada, the other taxes that arise on your death can still be substantial. Fortunately, with careful planning, you can reduce the taxes your estate will have to pay and increase the amount your beneficiaries will receive.

There are three types of tax that can be payable on your death:

- **Capital gains tax.** You are deemed to sell all of your capital property when you die, and your estate must pay the taxes on any capital gains, subject to a $500,000 lifetime exemption for capital gains from qualified small business shares and qualified farm property.
- **Tax on RRSP and RRIF assets.** Your tax-sheltered assets held in registered plans (such as Registered Retirement Savings Plans (RRSPs) and Registered Retirement Income Funds (RRIFs)) lose their tax-sheltered status at death, and their full value must be included in your final tax return.
- **Probate fees.** Courts in all provinces except for Alberta and Quebec charge probate fees to confirm the validity of your will. These fees are a percentage of the total value of the assets that pass under the will. In Ontario for example, the cost to your estate will be about 1.25 per cent of the asset value.

We will look at ways to defer or reduce each of these taxes separately.

CAPITAL GAINS TAXES

You can defer capital gains taxes by transferring capital property to your spouse on your death. The taxes are then deferred until your spouse disposes of the property or dies.

If you have capital property that you think will increase substantially in value, you may want to consider transferring ownership of those assets to your children now rather than later. This will allow you to defer the capital gains tax that arises on the asset after the date you transfer it until your child disposes of the asset, which may be many years away. However, you will have to pay taxes on any capital gains that arise to the date of the transfer.

Principal Residence Exemption

Your principal residence is exempt from any capital gains taxes owing on death. You can only have one principal residence, so if you own more than one residence — for example a house and a cottage — you should designate the residence with the greater amount of capital gains as your principal residence. If you own your principal residence jointly with another person, it will be rolled over to that person on your death without any tax consequences.

TAX ON RRSP AND RRIF ASSETS

On your death, you can transfer your RRSPs and RRIFs into your spouse's RRSP or RRIF (or sometimes a registered pension plan for a financially dependent child or grandchild) without any tax consequences. This defers the tax liability on those assets until your spouse (or child or grandchild) disposes of the assets or dies.

REDUCING PROBATE FEES

You can avoid paying probate fees by excluding certain assets from your estate. For example, if you designate named individuals as the beneficiaries of your life insurance policies rather than your estate, the life insurance proceeds will not form part of your estate and will not be included in the calculation of probate fees.

There are several other ways to exclude assets from your estate and reduce probate fees:

- Make your spouse the beneficiary of your RRSP or RRIF.
- Transfer your property to the intended beneficiary before your death.

- Hold assets like real property or bank accounts jointly with your spouse or child, so that the property passes automatically to them on your death without going through your estate.
- Create a living trust that gives you access to income or capital during your lifetime but passes directly to your beneficiaries on your death.
- Prepare multiple wills if you have assets in more than one jurisdiction.
- Prepare two wills, one that covers assets that require probate and one that covers assets that do not.

There are pitfalls to these strategies, so make sure you do not sacrifice your estate planning goals simply to reduce probate fees. For example, if you transfer your bank account into joint ownership with a spendthrift child, that child may drain the account while you are alive. In that situation, paying the probate fees would have been a small price to pay to protect your savings from your child.

OTHER TAX-REDUCTION STRATEGIES

There are several other tax-reduction strategies that you may want to consider in the course of your estate planning:

- **Buy permanent life insurance to cover your estate's expected tax liabilities**. Life insurance benefits generally are not taxable, and adequate life insurance means that your estate will not have to sell non-liquid assets, like recreational property, to cover its tax liabilities.
- **Make charitable gifts in your will**. If these gifts are substantial, your estate will receive a valuable tax credit that will be applied to your income in your year of death and the prior year.
- **Take advantage of unused RRSP contribution room**. If you have unused RRSP contribution room when you die and your spouse is aged 69 or younger, your executor can make a contribution to a spousal RRSP within 60 days of the end of year of your death. Your executor can them claim a deduction for the amount of the RRSP contribution on your terminal tax return.

In the next two chapters we will talk about two other important — and often more complex — tax-reduction strategies: the use of trusts and, if you own shares of a private corporation, estate freezes.

CHAPTER 9

TRUSTS

Trusts offer a number of benefits as an estate planning tool, from lowering or deferring taxes to providing a more flexible method of distributing assets. But before we look at the benefits, it is important to understand the basics of how trusts work.

A trust is created when you as the settlor transfer ownership of certain assets to a trustee who holds and manages the assets for the benefit of the beneficiaries. The beneficiaries are able to enjoy the benefits of the assets but do not legally own them. For example, if you transfer your cottage to your brother in trust for your children, your brother legally owns the cottage, but your children, and not your brother, are entitled to use the cottage.

Trusts can either be inter vivos trusts, which are created during your lifetime, or testamentary trusts, which are created in your will and take effect on your death. Different tax rules apply to the two types of trusts: inter vivos trusts are taxed at the highest marginal tax rate and testamentary trusts are subject to the graduated tax rates that apply to individuals.

There are many different types of trusts that may be useful as part of your estate plan. These include:

- **Income trusts.** You can create a trust that gives the beneficiaries the income earned by the trust's capital assets (like an investment account). For greater flexibility, the trustee may also be given the right to decide how much income should be paid to the beneficiaries. The trustee may also be given the right to pay part of the capital to the beneficiaries over a period of time.
- **Spendthrift trusts.** If you have a family member who does not handle money well or who has a history of financial problems, you may be concerned about giving this person access to a large sum of money. A spendthrift trust allows you

to ensure that the member has the income he or she needs, while preventing the person from depleting the capital.
- **Trusts for special needs beneficiaries.** If you have a child with special needs, you can use a trust to secure their long-term future. A special form of trust can be created to ensure that the child is not disqualified from receiving provincial disability support benefits.
- **Spousal trusts.** Transferring property to a trust for the benefit of your spouse allows you to defer the capital gains taxes that will arise on your death until the trust disposes of the property or your spouse dies.
- **Family trusts.** These are useful for income-splitting among family members, particularly if the family owns a business. We will look at these in more detail in Chapter 10.
- **Incentive trusts.** An incentive trust is used to motivate beneficiaries who expect to inherit a large amount of money to lead a productive life. We will discuss this type of trust in more detail at the end of this Chapter.

ADVANTAGES OF A TRUST

Trusts offer many advantages, both to the settlor and the beneficiaries:

- **Tax reduction.** Since testamentary trusts are taxed at the same graduated rates as individuals, they can be used to income-split among the beneficiaries. In addition, money can be distributed from the trust so as to minimize the tax consequences to the beneficiaries. For example, capital gains, which are taxed more favourably than other types of income, can be paid by the trust to the beneficiaries and taxed in their hands.
- **Protection from creditors.** Assets that are held in a trust are usually protected from the beneficiaries' creditors.
- **Money management.** If a child inherits a large sum of money at a young age, he or she may not be able to properly manage that money. If the money is held in a trust, the trustee can ensure that the child's living costs and other appropriate expenses are covered, but can delay distributing the bulk of the funds until the child is older and more financially responsible.

- **Gifts to minor children.** Children cannot legally own property until they reach the age of 18 years. If you want to leave assets to minor children, you must create a trust, or a provincially appointed Official Guardian or similar official will administer the money until the child turns 18.
- **Dispute resolution between children.** Transferring a contentious asset, like a cottage, to a trust for the benefit of your children allows the trustee to make decisions about that cottage and can reduce the conflict between your children.
- **Protection for a second spouse.** A trust can allow you to balance the needs of your children from your first marriage with the needs of a second spouse. You can transfer property to a trust that will provide income to your spouse during his or her lifetime. On your spouse's death, your children will receive the remaining capital from the trust.

CHOOSING YOUR TRUSTEE

You should choose a trustee as carefully as you choose an executor. Like your executor, the trustee should be someone you trust completely, as this person will be making important decisions about how money will be distributed to your family members. You may want to choose a family member or trusted friend who has the necessary skills to administer the trust. In certain circumstances, such as when the assets are very large or will be held over a long period of time, a professional trust company may be an appropriate choice.

You need to consider very carefully the powers you give the trustee to distribute capital and income to the beneficiaries. You can give your trustee complete discretion to make those decisions, or you can impose some restrictions on them (such as providing dates when the capital is to be distributed). In some cases, such as when the beneficiaries are quite young, giving the trustee broad discretionary powers may better allow your intentions to be carried out.

> **Trusts can Provide Much Needed Flexibility**
>
> Alison Deavers owned a printing business that had been founded by her father. She had three children, all of whom were in high school, and like her father, she wanted to keep the business in the family. However, her children were too young for her to determine if any of them were truly interested in running the business. Alison left the shares of her

> business to a trust that she set up in her will. She named her younger brother, to whom she often turned for business advice, as trustee and gave him the discretion to divide the shares of the business between the three children as he saw fit.
>
> Alison knows that at some point before she dies, she may determine that the trust is no longer appropriate. As her children grow older, she may decide how she wants the shares of her business disposed of on her death, particularly if one or more of the children have assumed an active role in the business. If that occurs, she will need to amend her will. But at this point in time, the trust that she has established in her will provides the best option for distributing her business shares should she die prematurely.

The trustee must act in an even-handed and impartial manner, both in investing the trust assets and in distributing those assets. The trustee is required to weigh the competing interests of both capital beneficiaries and income beneficiaries in making decisions about the trust.

For example, a beneficiary who is entitled to income from the trust might want the trust to invest in volatile stocks where there is a risk to the capital, but also potentially higher dividends, in order to increase their income stream. A beneficiary who is entitled to the capital of the trust might want the trust to invest in conservative investments like GICs, that earn a low return but create no risk to the capital.

In making investment decisions, trustees are governed by the "prudent investor" rule that requires the trustee to consider all options, canvass those options with a trained investment advisor, receive written advice from the investment advisor, and invest the assets in a prudent manner. In practice, trustees often invest about 60 per cent of the trust assets in equities and the remaining 40 per cent in low risk cash or bond type investments.

If you are creating a trust in your will, you will want to discuss both your choice of trustee and the powers you are giving them with your family members at the family conference. This is particularly true if you are giving the trustee broad discretionary powers. Your children may be less willing to accept decisions made by a trustee than decisions made by you, so it is important that they fully understand why you have given these powers to the trustee and that the trustee is someone they respect.

INCENTIVE TRUSTS

Incentive trusts are different from the other types of trusts used in estate planning because their primary purpose has little to do with the distribution of assets. Instead, they are intended to motivate "trust babies" into becoming financially self-sufficient, notwithstanding the fact that they may be the beneficiaries of a substantial trust.

Parents who know that their children will inherit a large amount of money have increasingly become worried about the dangers of "affluenza". They are concerned that children who expect a large inheritance may be disinclined to pursue higher education and may depend on the trust money rather than their personal resources. Parents may use an incentive trust to encourage certain types of productive behaviour from their children.

With an incentive trust, the trust rewards certain behaviour. For example, the trust may provide that the more money the child earns on her own, the more money he or she will receive from the trust. Or the trust can reward the child financially for attending university and achieving certain grades. The trust can also penalize the child for unacceptable behaviour. For example, the child could be denied money from the trust if he or she fails a drug test, but then be given money if the child enters a treatment program.

It is often difficult to draft the terms of incentive trusts because it is hard to anticipate all of the different types of desirable behaviour. For example, should stay-at-home parents be rewarded with extra income? What about someone who earns little money, but spends 20 hours a week volunteering for a charity? Tying specific benefits to specific behaviour makes the trust easier to administer, yet the language of the trust needs to be broad enough to include unknown future events.

If you are considering an incentive trust, you should think about both the broad and specific behaviours you want to encourage. If the behaviour you describe is too general or is difficult to evaluate, it will be hard for the trustee to administer the trust. Keep in mind that the goal of an incentive trust is to encourage the child to take responsibility for his or her own behaviour. In order for an incentive trust to work, the child must be motivated by money, and the person administering the trust must do so fairly with the ultimate goal of encouraging the child's independence.

Incentive trusts should be used in conjunction with open communication with your children about money. You should clearly discuss the financial arrangements you have made, and address the emotional issues that arise from the financial support you provide. Your children should clearly understand that your goals for them are to be financially independent and confident apart from their trust funds, and that they understand the value of achieving financial self-sufficiency.

At the same time, you may want to involve your children in making decisions about the trust's investments and distributions. Helping your children acquire financial knowledge is a valuable step in helping them achieve financial independence. As your children's maturity and financial knowledge increase, you may find that they are ready to handle the income and capital from the trust by themselves.

CHAPTER 10

ESTATE FREEZES

If you own a business that you intend to pass to your children, and you expect the business to increase in value, you can use an estate freeze to minimize the taxes that will be due on your death.

An estate freeze allows you to freeze the value of the shares of your company so that all future growth in the company's value will be for the benefit of your children. Since the value of your shares has been frozen, you know with certainty the amount of the taxes that will arise on your death and can make arrangements to pay that amount. And although your children will be responsible for the taxes that arise on the increase in value of the company after the date of transfer, they won't have to pay those taxes until they dispose of their shares or they die.

Here is one example of how an estate freeze can work. Assume you are the sole owner of the shares of a manufacturing company:

Manufacturing company	**Parent 100%**

You transfer your shares of the manufacturing company to a holding company, in exchange for preference shares of the holding company that have a redemption value equal to the fair market value of the manufacturing company. These shares should allow you to vote, so that you still have control over the company's decisions.

Your children buy common shares of the holding company for a nominal value. The holding company owns all of the shares of the manufacturing company:

Manufacturing Company	**Holding Company 100%**	
	Parent – voting preference shares	Children – common shares

The value of your preference shares is fixed, so those shares will be unaffected by any future growth of the operating company. Instead, any growth in the value of the operating company will increase the value of the common shares held by your children (through the holding company).

Although estate freezes are an extremely useful strategy for business owners in deferring taxes, one often overlooked complication is that the founder of the company, who is used to complete autonomy in running the business, loses some business control. This is true even if the shares of the holding company that the founder takes back have voting rights. When the founder's loss of control is combined with sometimes difficult parent-child family dynamics, litigation can result.

Letting Go of Control

Bill Smith has run his own small car parts company for 25 years. He has enjoyed having his son Jim and daughter Linda working with him during the last five years and has given them each common shares in the business. However, lately family relationships have been growing increasingly strained.

Jim is buying an expensive cottage and Linda is getting married. Both children need to draw more money from the company to support their new lifestyles. Bill has been reluctant to let them do so because the company will then have to borrow funds, which it hasn't done in years.

Bill receives a letter from Jim's and Linda's lawyer demanding full disclosure of the company's books and records, which is their statutory right as shareholders. Bill is used to running the company as he wishes, and is angry at his children for retaining a lawyer. Although he tries meeting with Jim and Linda to discuss their concerns, the meeting is heated and they are unable to reach a resolution. Soon they are barely speaking to each other.

Bill decides to use a third party mediator to hold a series of family conferences to work through the issues. Bill knows that his children have a legal right to the information they are requesting and his children know that disclosure of the information does not mean they will necessarily receive more money from the company. The mediator is able to help all three address the financial and emotional tensions that have arisen before the economic viability of the company is threatened.

Since the children now hold common shares of the holding company, they are entitled to various rights set out in the statutes governing business corporations. For example, they have the right to receive audited financial statements of the corporation and to attend an annual shareholders' meeting. Prior to the estate freeze, the company founder likely ran the company without scrutiny from anyone, and he or she may find the new structure difficult to fully accept. For this reason, an estate freeze often works better if it is done in conjunction with the implementation of a business succession plan in which the founder gives up day-to-day control of the business.

USE OF FAMILY TRUSTS

If the company founder wants to proceed with an estate freeze, but still wants to preserve control over the business, then he or she may want to consider transferring the common shares of the holding company to a family trust for the benefit of the children rather than to the children themselves. The trustees can be the company founder and the founder's trusted advisors.

Manufacturing Company	Holding Company 100%	
	Trustees – Parent and Advisors	Family trust for benefit of children

The use of the family trust in an estate freeze has a number of potential advantages:

- The founder has greater control over the common shares through his or her role as trustee.
- The children will not become the legal owners of the shares until the trust document so provides.
- The trustees controls the disposition of income from the company.
- The trust allows all children, even those not involved with the company, to share in its growth.

CHAPTER 11

POWER OF ATTORNEY

A power of attorney allows you to plan for situations where you may become incapacitated and unable to make decisions about your property or your health. With a power of attorney, you appoint another person (known as the "attorney", although the person does not have to be a lawyer) to make those decisions on your behalf. A power of attorney is only effective during your lifetime and terminates on your death.

There are two different types of power of attorney: a power of attorney for property, which allows the attorney to manage your property for you, and a power of attorney for personal care, which allows the attorney to make health care decisions for you if you become incapable of making those decisions. You do not have to appoint the same person to both positions.

Both types of power of attorney must be signed in the presence of two witnesses. They cannot be your spouse, any of your children, the person being appointed as attorney, nor that person's spouse. You can also revoke the power of attorney by signing a revocation in the presence of two witnesses.

POWER OF ATTORNEY FOR PROPERTY

A power of attorney for property is a written document in which you give your attorney the authority to make decisions on your behalf about your property, including your bank accounts, investments, real estate and other assets.

A power of attorney for property normally specifies that it does not take effect until the person who granted the power becomes mentally incapacitated. However, you can also grant a power of attorney for another specified purpose and which is effective for only that purpose and, usually, only for a limited period of time. For example, if you are selling your house and your spouse is going to be out of town during the time that offers to purchase are expected, your spouse could appoint you to act as his or her attorney during that time period.

Mental Capacity Required

Just as you need the proper mental capacity to execute a will, you must have the proper mental capacity to give a power of attorney for property. In order to have mental capacity, you must:

- Know what kind of property you have and its approximate value.
- Be aware of the obligations that you may owe to your dependants.
- Know that the attorney can do anything with your property that you could do, other than make a will, subject to the conditions set out in the power of attorney document.
- Know that you may revoke the power of attorney, if you are capable.

It can be difficult to subsequently determine whether or not someone had the necessary capacity to sign a power of attorney at the time it was signed. As with your will, if you have any concerns that your capacity may later be challenged, make sure your lawyer takes detailed notes of your instructions and consider asking your family doctor to make a formal assessment of your capacity.

If you become incapacitated and you do not have a power of attorney, the court will appoint someone to act on your behalf. This may not be the person you would have chosen.

Restrictions

A power of attorney for property is usually drafted without any restrictions on the authority of the attorney. The attorney can act on your behalf for all of your financial matters. The attorney can do anything with your property that you could do, other than make a will.

There may be situations, however, where a limited power of attorney is more appropriate. For example, an elderly person who has difficulty going to the bank might appoint one of his or her children as attorney solely to deposit and withdraw money from the bank, but not give that child the authority to carry out any other financial transactions on her behalf.

The downside of a limited power of attorney is that if you become incapacitated, it will not allow your attorney to manage all of your affairs. For that reason, if you have a limited power of attorney, you should also sign another one that does not contain any restrictions on the attorney's ability to act, and deposit it with your lawyer or someone else you trust with instructions not to release it until you become incapacitated.

Choice of Attorney

The most important decision you will make when preparing a power of attorney for property is who to appoint as your attorney. Because your attorney will have complete authority over your financial affairs while you are still alive, you must have absolute trust in the person you appoint. You are giving that person a blank cheque, so consider your choice very carefully and be very cautious about releasing the document. You may want to consider depositing the power of attorney with your lawyer with instructions that it should only be released if a medical certificate of your incapacity is obtained.

The choice of attorney can create an emotional rift within a family, particularly if you choose one child over another. While you may have chosen one child for purely practical reasons (he or she lives near you and have the time necessary to manage your affairs), your other children may feel that your decision means that you favour that child. This type of misunderstanding may lead to costly litigation. I will discuss challenges to a power of attorney for property in more detail below.

In some situations, it may be appropriate to appoint joint attorneys, particularly if you are choosing between your children and the choice is likely to be contentious.

> **Joint Attorney Can be an Effective Solution**
>
> Doris Levy is an elderly widow with two children. Although she is mentally competent, she finds it very difficult to get around and she does not like dealing with financial matters, all of which had been handled by her late husband. Although she wants one of her two children to manage her affairs, she is unsure which one to appoint. Her daughter has a history of making rash investments, and Doris is concerned that she might do the same with her money. She feels that her son is completely trustworthy, but he does not have the time to manage her day-to-day banking transactions.
>
> Doris decides to appoint her children as joint attorneys for her property. The power of attorney document provides that either child

> can separately make withdrawals or write cheques in amounts up to $500, but that both children must jointly approve any other decision. By structuring her power of attorney this way, Doris gives her daughter the ability to manage her ordinary banking transactions, but ensures that her son will be involved in major decisions. She also ensures that there will be no animosity between her two children because of her choice of attorney.

You may also want to consider appointing a neutral person or a financial institution to act as your attorney in order to reduce the family tension and limit the likelihood of potential court challenges. However, many people are unwilling to consider appointing a neutral party for two reasons:

- **Family control**: There is often comfort in leaving financial decision-making in the hands of family members. However, many people rely heavily on their own professional advisors, such as financial planners, lawyers and accountants, to either run or assist in running their financial affairs while they have the capacity to make their own decisions. One of those people would be equally capable of acting during incapacity. In addition, financial institutions are not only neutral parties; they are experienced in the fiduciary administration process and able to satisfy the obligations of an attorney.
- **Cost**: Many people are worried that appointing a neutral party will be unnecessarily costly. In most jurisdictions, an attorney is entitled to receive compensation of approximately 5 per cent – 6 per cent of the assets that the attorney administers, although you can negotiate a different rate. Many family members volunteer to act as attorney without compensation, so appointing a neutral party appears far less attractive. However, there is a tremendous amount of work involved in properly acting as an attorney, so the fee should be paid to anyone who is prepared to take on the job, even if that person is a family member.

Your adult children may initially be opposed to the appointment of a neutral third party as your attorney. However, once they fully understand the obligations that arise from acting as an attorney, and in particular the amount of time the job will take, they generally welcome the opportunity to give the job to a professional.

CHALLENGES TO A POWER OF ATTORNEY FOR PROPERTY

There are numerous grounds on which family members can challenge a power of attorney for property, and if they are unhappy with the choice of attorney, it will not be difficult for them to find such grounds. For example, if the power of attorney was prepared shortly before the finding of incapacity, family members may claim that you lacked capacity when you appointed the attorney and were pressured to do so by the attorney. Or the family members can challenge the accounts of the attorney or scrutinize his or her every action so that it is difficult for the attorney to effectively administer your assets.

Family members have a legitimate interest in ensuring that the attorney behaves appropriately. They want to make certain that the person granting the power of attorney has enough money to live comfortably during his or her lifetime and that the attorney does not erode the assets the family members will receive under the will. However, family dynamics and hurt feelings can exacerbate the legitimate concerns of the family members and make the attorney's role extremely complicated.

One particular problem that often arises stems from the right of the attorney to look at the will. Attorneys are entitled to view the will so that in administering the estate, they are aware of its ultimate disposition. While this information can be very useful to an attorney who is developing an investment plan, it can also create family tension. The attorney is not supposed to disclose the provisions of the will to anyone unless absolutely necessary, but often details leak out and problems arise. This situation can be prevented if you hold a family conference in which you discuss the terms of your will with your family members so that they are not surprised by its contents.

You should also discuss your power of attorney for property at the family conference. Even families who spend a great deal of time on the family conference process in connection with the will often fail to consider the power of attorney. Because of the expansive role of the attorney and the effect of his or her decisions on the estate plan, it is essential to have a full discussion with your family members about the plans you have made if you become incapacitated.

POWER OF ATTORNEY FOR PERSONAL CARE

A power of attorney for personal care allows you to appoint an attorney to make decisions about your personal health care if you become incapable of making those decisions.

This document is sometimes called a living will or an advance health care directive. Your attorney is allowed to make decisions on your behalf about your medical and health care, nutrition, shelter, clothing, hygiene and safety. You can include specific instructions to your attorney about the decisions that they will make on your behalf (such as refusing unnecessary measures to prolong your life if you have a terminal illness).

If you become incapacitated, medical professionals will consult with your attorney to obtain instructions on your care. In selecting an attorney, you should choose someone who understands your personal wishes and who will convey those wishes to the professionals involved. If you desire, you can appoint joint powers of attorney who must make decisions together about your personal care.

Although a person must have the mental capacity to give a power of attorney for personal care, the level of capacity required is much lower than that required to give a power of attorney for property. You are capable of giving a power of attorney for personal care if you:

- have the ability to understand whether the proposed attorney has a genuine concern for your personal welfare and
- appreciate that you may need to have the proposed attorney make decisions for you.

Because your attorney for personal care does not handle any of your money or financial affairs, your family members are less likely to challenge your choice than they are to challenge your attorney for property. However, it is still a good idea to discuss your choice of attorney with your family members at the family conference and to ensure that the whole family is aware of any specific instructions you have given your attorney as to the treatment you do or do not want to receive.

Part 2

Why Estate Plans are Challenged — And What it Costs

CHAPTER 12

TEN MOST FREQUENT CAUSES OF ESTATE LITIGATION

Even if you have a comprehensive, professionally drafted plan, your estate can still become the subject of litigation. And while you will not be around when the dispute occurs, there are good reasons for taking an interest now in ensuring an estate battle does not happen.

Estate litigation often leaves a great deal of both emotional and financial heartache. After carefully ensuring that your loved ones are taken care of in your estate plan, the last thing you want is a fight over it, and even worse, having it restructured so that your wishes are ignored. You also do not want to leave a legacy of emotional strife and ruined relationships within the family.

The first step toward avoiding an estate dispute is understanding the most frequent causes of estate litigation. In the next Chapter, we will look at the costs of the litigation process, to further illustrate the value that a professionally-mediated family conference can bring.

TEN MOST FREQUENT CAUSES

In my opinion, here are the ten most common causes of estate litigation.

1. **Lack of Understanding on the need for an estate plan**
   Ignorance may be bliss in some situations, but when it comes to estate planning, you will pay a high price if you do not understand the need for a proper plan. Many people die without knowing what an estate plan could have accomplished, or the disputes it might have prevented.

2. **Estate plan is not current**
   If your personal circumstances or your intentions for your estate change, it is essential that your will and powers of attorney be updated to reflect your new circumstances. If any of the following circumstances occur, you should review your estate plan to see if changes are necessary:

- One of your principal beneficiaries dies.
- You marry, divorce or remarry.
- A child or grandchild is born.
- You have an extramarital relationship.
- One of your beneficiaries or dependants becomes disabled.
- The value of your assets significantly increases or decreases.
- You receive an unexpected inheritance.
- You sell a significant asset, including your business, family home or recreational property.
- Your beneficiaries under your RRSPs, pension plans or insurance polices are redesignated or have their entitlements change.
- You establish a secret trust.
- You experience a change in your business (for example, your partnership dissolves or you incorporate a company).
- Tax or other legislative changes occur that affect your estate plan.

3. **Inadequate estate planning advice**

   Do not rely on second-class advice if you want to avoid legal problems and estate litigation. Look for an estate planning professional (usually a lawyer, accountant, financial planner or insurance professional) who has experience with your type of personal situation. A proper estate plan can take time, so if your situation has any complexities (difficult family situation, assets outside of Canada, private business ownership) avoid anyone claiming to have a quick estate solution.

4. **Reluctance to seek advice**

   While it is natural to be reluctant to obtain professional estate planning advice, your family will suffer if you are unable to overcome this reluctance and prepare a carefully considered estate plan. The only valid reason for not preparing an estate plan is if you are comfortable with how your property will be disposed of by law — and that very rarely occurs.

5. **Acrimonious extended family**

   If your extended family is acrimonious, the best way to avoid litigation is to ensure that the estate plan is as enforceable as possible. This means making certain that all necessary separation, marriage, cohabitation, partnership, employment and shareholders' agreements that may affect your estate are in place before you die. When you are considering your extended family, you need to include your spouse and any former spouses (legal or common law), your children and their spouses and former spouses (legal or common law), your grandchildren and their spouses and former spouses (legal or common law), your siblings, nieces and nephews, your extramarital partners and any other dependants, whether related to you or not. Any one of those people might bring an action against your estate.

6. **Frailties and secrets**

If you have kept secrets from your family, such as an extramarital relationship, an undisclosed illness or mental or physical illnesses that are not known by your family until after your death, problems often arise. Unless you have provided for these claims in a secret trust, unjustified demands may be made against your estate. For example, you may have a nephew making an extended visit from overseas who takes you to your medical appointments and goes grocery shopping for you. Although your family members think your nephew is just being kind to you during his time in the country, your nephew secretly expects to receive an inheritance from you when you die, and may make a claim against your estate.

7. **Intransigent family members**

When family members become involved in an estate dispute, the intense feelings that arise are often as bitter as those in matrimonial disputes. Family members may take positions that are completely unreasonable and be resistant to their advisors' more rational advice. This often continues through to the pretrial stage of litigation where the admonitions of the judge generally play a positive role in encouraging negotiation.

8. **Poorly drafted documents**

Poorly drafted documents can create enormous problems for an estate. These include documents that:

- Contain clauses that are unclear, so that the intention of the person making the document is difficult to determine.
- Contain intricate provisions that become ineffective or unwise over time.
- Do not anticipate contingencies that later occur.

You can usually prevent poor drafting by having your estate planning documents prepared by reputable, experienced professionals.

9. **Nature of the assets**

    The mix and nature of the assets and the way you dealt with them during your lifetime can create problems. For example, if you have failed to redesignate a beneficiary for your RRSP when the original beneficiary died, you may have created unnecessary complications and costs for your estate. Similarly, if your major asset is a cottage or a small company that has high accrued capital gains, your family members will need enough cash to pay for the tax liabilities that will arise on your death, or they may be forced to sell the asset to generate the necessary funds. If the asset has strong emotional significance, like a family cottage, your family may be very reluctant to sell it. This problem can be avoided if you buy sufficient life insurance to cover the tax liability expected on your death.

10. **Actions of personal representatives**

    The executors and trustees appointed under your will must be scrupulously fair. It is important that they set aside any pre-existing feelings and prejudices they have about the estate or the beneficiaries. Family members will be closely scrutinizing their actions, particularly during the period immediately after they have been appointed. If the executors and trustees are able to establish good relationships with family members at the beginning of their appointments, they will usually be able to successfully administer the estate.

While these ten factors often motivate family members to challenge a will, they cannot form the legal basis for a claim by themselves. You cannot bring a claim against your father's estate on the basis that he was having a long-term extramarital relationship. However, if you are angry with your father for having the relationship and upset that he has left money to his girlfriend, you might look for a legal basis to challenge his will. For example, you might decide to make a dependants' relief claim against his estate on the basis that your father had a legal obligation to support you that was not adequately met in his will. The court would then make a determination of that claim.

CLAIMS AGAINST THE WILL

You need a legal basis to challenge a will. In general, there are four types of claims that can be made against a will:

- Dependants' relief claims.
- *Family Law Act* claims.
- Breach of contract claims.
- Constructive trust claims.

These claims are different from claims that the will is invalid, which we discussed in Chapter 4. These claims accept the validity of the will, but argue that the deceased did not provide adequately for the claimant and that the provisions affecting the claimant should be amended. A claim that the will is invalid seeks to strike down the whole will, which is then replaced by either an earlier prior will or by intestacy provisions set out in provincial laws.

DEPENDANTS' RELIEF CLAIMS

Succession laws in every province allow persons to make dependants' relief claims against estates. Typically, in order to make such a claim, the person must fall within the statutory definition of dependant, which would include a spouse (including common-law and same-sex partners), parent, child, grandchild or sibling of the deceased. The deceased must either have been providing financial support to the person immediately before death, or have been under a legal obligation to do so (such as a parent who has been legally ordered to pay child support but who is not actually doing so).

The dependants' relief provisions allow people who meet the test for "dependants" to claim that the deceased has not adequately provided for their support. If the court is satisfied with the claim, it may order that the person is entitled to a share (or an increased share) of the assets of the estate.

In determining whether this type of claim will succeed, court uses a two-step process. The first step is to assess whether the person is a dependant and if so, whether that person shows financial need. If the first step is satisfied, the second step is to determine how much support should be awarded. A variety of factors will be considered, including the nature of the dependant's relationship with the deceased, the length of the relationship and the dependant's future earnings prospects. It will also look at the moral considerations and will divide the assets, in part, so that the dependant receives a "fair share" of the estate.

You need to consider all possible claims that could be made by your dependants. For example, you may be sending $250 a month to your brother overseas. Because this amount is relatively small and you are sending it voluntarily, you may not consider it when you are preparing your estate plan. However, after your death your brother might file a dependants' relief claim against your estate.

Family Law Entitlements

In most provinces, a "community of property" regime exists for couples that are legally married (it does not apply to common law spouses). This means that, under family and succession laws, if a marriage ends by either divorce or death, the two spouses are entitled to share equally in the value of the property and assets acquired *during the marriage*, whether or not they contributed equally to such assets.

For example, in Ontario, when one spouse dies, the other spouse can either take his or her inheritance under the will, or can choose to take his or her entitlement under provincial family law. The spouse will likely choose to take his or her entitlement under family law if it is more favourable than his or her treatment in the will. You should keep the provisions of applicable family laws in mind when you are drafting your will to ensure that you do not leave your spouse less than they would be entitled to under those laws.

Factor in Family Law Impact

Adrian Wong lives in Ontario. When her husband David died, he left Adrian with assets valued at $500,000 under his will, with the remainder of his assets divided between their three children and his favourite charity. When they were married, they each had assets valued at $25,000 and had no liabilities. At the time of his death, after deducting their respective debts, David owned assets worth $800,000, while Adrian owned assets worth $200,000.

The value of David's net family property at his death was $775,000 ($800,000 less the $25,000 he had when they married). The value of Adrian's net family property at David's death was $175,000 ($200,000 less the $25,000 she had when they married). The difference in the value of their net family property is $600,000 ($775,000 - $175,000). Adrian can elect to take either one-half of that ($300,000), or she can take the $500,000 David left her in his will, which is obviously the choice she would make.

However, if David had assets of $1.5 million at his death, the difference in the value of their net family property would be $1.3 million. Adrian would be entitled to one-half of that, or $650,000,

> under Ontario's *Family Law Act* (R.S.O. 1990, c. F.3), which would be preferable to the $500,000 she was left under David's will.

Breach of Contract

You can also make a claim for breach of contract or *quantum meruit* against the estate if you provided work or services to the deceased while that person was alive. If the deceased promised to pay you a certain amount of money for your services, but never did, you could make a claim for breach of contract. Even if no specific amount of money had been agreed upon, you could still make a *quantum meruit* claim, being a claim for a reasonable amount for your work or services.

You can also make a claim for breach of contract against the estate if the deceased simply promised you money, for whatever reason, to be paid on his or her death.

Constructive Trust

You can also claim that the deceased was holding assets in trust for you, and that one-half of the estate should be distributed to you notwithstanding the provisions of the will. This is known as a constructive trust claim, and has been popular among common-law couples, who are not entitled to make equalization claims under provincial family laws. Courts may take the view that if a couple has lived together for a long time period and jointly accumulated assets, those assets should be equally split between the parties regardless of which partner actually bought them.

CHAPTER 13

THE LEGAL PROCESS AND ITS COSTS

Estate litigation can be enormously costly, both financially and emotionally. People generally focus on the financial costs of estate litigation, but the emotional costs can be just as high — and can last forever. Estate litigation is usually bitter and divisive, and family members may become permanently estranged. The use of a family conference to solve disputes before they become litigious can protect your family from all of these costs.

WHAT ARE LEGAL COSTS?

Legal costs are the fees and disbursements you pay to your lawyer. Traditionally, so long as the person challenging the will had good reason to do so, the estate has been ordered to pay the costs of all of the parties involved in litigation, regardless of who was successful in the action. This is because the person making the will is typically seen as causing the legal problem, either by using a poorly drafted will or by disinheriting beneficiaries for no apparent reason.

However, in recent years courts have been moving away from requiring the estate to pay all the litigation costs. In awarding costs, courts are increasingly considering the success the parties achieve in the litigation, which means that people may have to bear their own costs or that a person who unsuccessfully challenges the will may be ordered to pay the estate's costs.

Even when the court orders that costs be paid, you may still be left with a substantial legal bill. Courts usually order that costs be paid on a partial indemnity basis, which means that somewhere between only 30 per cent and 60 per cent of the actual lawyer's fees and disbursements will be covered. Courts will only order costs to be paid on a substantial indemnity basis, which generally covers 100 per cent of the legal costs, only when they want to show their disapproval of the conduct of one of the parties or their lawyers.

STAGES IN A COURT ACTION

There are several stages in any estate litigation, and your costs will climb as you move through each stage.

Stage 1 — Order Organizing the Litigation

The first stage in challenging a will is to file an objection to the will with the court and to obtain a court order that will identify the parties and give directions as to what issues the litigation will determine. The order may also appoint someone to administer the estate during the litigation.

Obtaining this court order generally will cost between $5,000 and $10,000.

Stage 2 — Collecting and Disclosing Evidence

In the second stage, you will need to locate and collect all the records you need to establish your case. This requires contacting all of the deceased's medical professionals, financial institutions and advisors and serving them with a court order requiring them to provide copies of their notes. This task can be extremely daunting because the deceased may have had appointments with many different doctors, nurses, social workers and other health care professionals. In many cases these professionals will charge a fee for providing their notes. In addition, you may not be familiar with all of the deceased's bank or investment accounts, and may have to spend time locating them before you are able to obtain the information you need.

Collecting the documents usually takes between three and nine months, and may cost between $1,000 and $10,000, depending on the complexity of the estate.

After the documents are collected, you will need to prepare and file a formal affidavit of documents listing and describing in detail each document on which you are relying. Preparing the affidavit of documents will cost between $1,000 and $10,000, depending on the number of documents you need to disclose.

Stage 3 — Discoveries

The next stage in litigation is the discovery process, which many people know as "taking depositions". During this stage, the parties give evidence under oath and are cross-examined by the other party's lawyer about that evidence. Transcripts are taken of their testimony for use at trial. The purpose of discoveries is to allow each party to review all of the evidence to determine the strengths and weaknesses of their respective cases, and to make a realistic assessment of his or her likelihood of success.

The discovery process can be very time-consuming and financially and emotionally draining. The parties can expect to be aggressively questioned at length by the opposing lawyer who is trying to test both the strength of his or her case and how strong a witness each party will make at trial.

This is usually an expensive stage of litigation, second only to the trial itself. While it is impossible to accurately estimate the costs of discoveries, costs will generally start at $10,000 and increase from there. In addition, the costs of the transcripts can be considerable. A typical deposition will generate a transcript that is 200 pages in length, with each page costing between $2.00 to $3.50.

Stage 4 — Pre-trial Conference

At the pre-trial conference, a judge (who is then not permitted to be the trial judge) will act as a mediator and try to help the parties reach a settlement. Although the pre-trial conference is relatively informal, it is essential that the lawyers be well prepared for it to be useful, and both parties are required to prepare memos outlining their cases.

After reading the memos and hearing the lawyers outline their positions, the pre-trial judge will give an opinion on how the issues will likely be determined at trial. This can provide the parties with a more realistic perspective on the strength of their cases.

The pre-trial conference will generally cost between $3,000 and $7,500.

Stage 5 — Trial

If no settlement has been reached, a trial will take place. This is usually the most expensive and most difficult stage in the litigation process. Each side calls witnesses who testify before a judge, who then decides the case. If the trial lasts for more than a day or two, the judge will usually prepare written reasons for his or her decision, which are made public.

The judge's decision on the case is final, subject to appeal. Most people find the experience of discussing personal family matters in an open courtroom to be extremely upsetting. This is compounded by the fact that your testimony will be challenged by the opposing party's lawyer and then scrutinized and evaluated for truthfulness by a judge, who may comment on your actions or your testimony in his or her decision. The fact that the judge's decision is a public document, which can be accessed by anyone including your friends and acquaintances, makes the experience much worse for most people.

The costs of a trial are usually extremely high, and even the winner is unlikely to recover all of his or her costs. The exact amount will depend on how many lawyers are representing you, the amount of preparation time they require (which can range from 20 hours to hundreds of hours for each lawyer involved) and the number of expert witnesses who testify on your behalf. In general, trial costs will range from $15,000 to $30,000 a day, plus fees for preparation time.

Stage 6 — Appeal

Either party can appeal the decision of the trial judge. If you want to do so, you will need to order the trial transcripts so that you can prepare the necessary legal documents. Depending on the length of the trial, transcripts can cost from $5,000 to tens of thousands of dollars and may take months to be prepared. If you are appealing on a legal issue alone and there are no facts in dispute, you may not need the transcripts, but this is not the case in most estate litigation. Once the transcripts are ready, your lawyers need to prepare factums, which are summaries of the facts and law of the case, to be filed with the appeal court.

It can be very expensive to appeal a trial judge's decision. Costs will start at about $40,000 and increase from there. Appellate courts have the power to order costs, but there is even more uncertainty as to the payment of costs at that level. For example, if you win at trial and lose on appeal, the appeal court might order you to pay all the costs of both the trial and the appeal.

MEDIATION

Mediation is a non-binding process through which parties are encouraged to reach an agreement on the issues between them. Mediation is an excellent tool in estate matters as many of the issues can be readily resolved with the help of a trained mediator. If the mediation is effective, it has two main benefits:

- It costs far less than proceeding through the litigation process to trial.
- The parties are more likely to be satisfied with an agreement they have reached themselves than with a decision imposed on them by a judge.

Mediation also offers the parties privacy and confidentiality and it can be completed far more quickly than using the court process.

Mediation can be used before the parties begin litigation, or at any stage in the litigation process. In some jurisdictions, mediation is mandatory before the parties can go to trial.

The parties to a mediation sign an agreement that provides that everything said is confidential and cannot later be used in court if the mediation fails. The mediator's role is to facilitate a resolution to the dispute, not to give legal advice or impose a solution. If a settlement is reached, the parties sign binding minutes of settlement.

Although mediation can be far less costly than litigation, it is still an expensive process. An experienced mediator costs between $2,000 and $7,000 a day, and your lawyer will also have to prepare a legal mediation brief and attend the session with you. Mediation costs range from $7,500 to $25,000, which is money well spent if you are able to reach an agreement. However, if the mediation is unsuccessful, you will have to pay both the mediation costs and the litigation costs, which will add to your financial burden.

PART 3

THE FAMILY CONFERENCE SOLUTION

CHAPTER 14

FAMILY CONSTITUTIONS

In Part 1 of this book, we examined the basic components of estate planning — wills, tax reduction strategies and powers of attorney. In Part 2, we looked at the most common reasons family members have for challenging an estate plan, and the costs, both emotional and financial, of the litigation process.

In this final section, we discuss how you can use a professionally-mediated family conference to obtain the beneficiaries' approval of your estate plan through the signing of a family constitution.

A family constitution sets out the framework for both the estate plan (which then needs to be implemented by the family lawyer) and the process of ongoing family conferences and dispute resolution.

A family constitution is a private family document not intended to be widely circulated before your death, although your lawyer and other professional advisors will need to see it. If necessary, it may also be used to resolve disputes either within the family or through the courts. Because family constitutions include an agreement not to contest the will, they can be very effective in preventing estate litigation.

INTRODUCTORY WORDING

Introductions to family constitutions purposely use grand language to express the importance of these documents and the sincerity of the family in signing them. Samples of some of the introductory wording that may be included in a family constitution are set out below:

THE FAMILY CONSTITUTION FOR THE GORDON FAMILY

WHEREAS the Gordon Family knows that it is both healthy and natural for family members to hold different views and opinions, and that because of the complexities of life they need a system of family

governance and, to the extent that it is possible, joint or consultative decision-making;

WHEREAS the Gordon Family has unanimously decided to create a Family Constitution to assist with their primary goal of maintaining family peace and family harmony;

WHEREAS the Gordon Family acknowledge by their signatures below that they will abide by and follow the principles set out in the Family Constitution and that they will continue to work together to preserve the tremendous emotional and financial capital that has been created, preserved and maintained by the Gordon Family;

WHEREAS the Gordon Family knows and understands that their Family Constitution is a living document that requires patience and wisdom to preserve, use and enforce;

This introductory wording can be tailored to reflect the particular values and principles specific to your family.

WORDING OF FAMILY CONSTITUTION

Following the introduction, the family constitution should include all agreements reached at the family conference. It should contain clauses:

- Outlining the details of the estate plan that have been approved by all family members, including the choice of executor.
- Agreeing to use alternate dispute resolution techniques, like further family conferences or mediation, to resolve disputes between family members and the estate.
- Agreeing not to litigate upon your death provided no major changes are made to your estate plan.
- Agreeing to adjust the beneficiaries' entitlements to give effect to the spirit of the family constitution if you significantly change your estate plan after the family constitution is signed.
- Requiring you to provide continuing disclosure to your family members about the implementation of the estate plan and any issues that arise in the implementation process that may effect their entitlements under the estate plan.

The family constitution can be prepared and signed at the conclusion of the family conference. It gives everyone at the meeting a document to take with them that reflects the positive nature of the agreements made that day.

In some cases, family members may ask to have some time to consider the terms of the family constitution, or obtain their own legal advice, before signing it, and those wishes should be respected. However, it is important that the approval of the family constitution not be postponed indefinitely, so a subsequent family conference should be scheduled for signing the family constitution.

To be effective, a family constitution, like all constitutions, must be a living document. This means that it should be amended whenever circumstances change or the need arises. For example, if your estate plan changes significantly, you will need to amend that part of your family constitution. At each subsequent family conference, you should consider whether changes have occurred, either in the nature of your family or in the agreements made by your family, which affect the family constitution and require its amendment.

CHAPTER 15

BEFORE THE CONFERENCE

There are a number of steps you need to take before the family conference takes place to ensure that it runs smoothly. Naturally, your draft estate plan should be completed before you schedule a meeting. You will also need to:

- Decide who to invite.
- Prepare an agenda for the meeting.
- Appoint a chairperson.

WHO TO INVITE

You should invite all of the adult members of your family who are affected by your estate plan to the family conference. In some cases, there may be non-family members who should also be included. For example, if you have been supporting someone who is not related to you, it may be appropriate to invite that person.

At a minimum, your spouse and your children should attend the meeting. If you have adult grandchildren, they too should attend. In some cases, your siblings and possibly your nieces and nephews should attend. It may also be appropriate to include in-laws at the meeting.

> **Tailor Your Invitation List to Your Situation**
>
> Allan Tanaka is the sole owner of a freight forwarding business. He has two children, Gary and Neil, both of whom are married. Allan's son Gary works for the business, as does Allan's niece Kara. Allan's wife, Susan, has a child from a previous marriage, Ted, to whom Allan has provided money over the years, most recently two years ago when Ted needed help buying a home.
>
> Allan has decided to leave all the shares of the business to Gary. He intends to leave stocks and bonds with a value equal to that of the business to Neil. He is leaving his wife their home and cottage and a

> sizeable insurance policy. He is providing a $20,000 bequest to each of Ted and Kara.
>
> Allan should invite the following people to the family conference: his wife, their two children, their two daughters-in-law, his stepson and his niece. Any one of these people may potentially have a claim against the estate, so Allan needs to obtain their commitment to his estate plan.

Once you have decided which family members to invite, you need to consider how to invite them. If possible, speak first to your family members to explain the purpose of the conference and to find out when they will be available. The mediator can then send them a formal written invitation that includes the time and place of the meeting, who will be in attendance, and the agenda.

The office of the mediator is generally a good choice for the conference because it is a neutral location and will have conference rooms of various sizes, so that the whole family can meet together but also break into smaller caucus groups if necessary.

Using your home as the location for the family conference is generally not advisable. First, it is not a neutral location and family arguments are more likely to develop. Second, it is too easy for the conference to turn into a social event. Holding the conference elsewhere encourages the family members to focus on the issues at hand and to treat it with the same professional attitude they would treat a business meeting.

It is important that all family members attend in person, especially at the first meeting, so that they are able to fully participate in the discussion on the proposed estate plan. If a family member is absolutely unable to attend because he or she lives too far away, arrangements can be made to include that member by telephone conference. That said, the use of telephone conferencing should be reserved for brief subsequent meetings that do not warrant extensive travel.

In some cases, despite your best efforts, family members may be unwilling to discuss your proposed estate plan and refuse to attend the meeting. We will discuss the partially attended family conference in more detail in Chapter 17.

MINOR CHILDREN

Children under the age of 18 usually do not attend family conferences because they have no direct role in the transfer of wealth in a family. However, you need to consider whether the implementation of the estate plan may have an impact on their interests. Every province has a branch of government that is responsible for protecting the financial interests of minor children (in Ontario, for example, it is the Office of the Children's Lawyer). That government branch may object to changes made to an existing estate plan that includes fixed gifts to minor children. Your lawyer can help you decide whether the government should be involved in the estate planning process or the family conference.

PREPARING THE AGENDA

The preparation of an agenda in advance of the family conference ensures that all of the issues you want addressed at the conference are both raised and discussed in an order that you think is appropriate.

Before the conference, the mediator should meet with you and your lawyer to become both familiar with the estate plan and aware of issues that may be contentious. This will allow the mediator to be prepared for the concerns of the family members that may be raised at the conference, and to consider possible solutions. The mediator will then work with you to prepare the agenda.

Many people find it helpful to have the agenda follow the format of the estate plan. This allows for a logical order of the conference that essentially follows your wishes as expressed in the estate plan. Organizing the agenda in this way helps maintain a businesslike environment for the meeting and encourages the discussion to remain focused on the details of the estate plan.

Noted below is a draft that I use as a starting point when I meet with the head of a family to prepare an agenda tailored to his or her specific needs:

FAMILY CONFERENCE AGENDA

1. Introduction

    - background regarding the mediator (**mediator**)

    - summary of the family conference process (**mediator**)

2. Overview of overall estate plan (**mediator**)

3. Opening statements (**head of family**)

4. Detailed review of proposed estate plan (**family lawyer**)

   a. Current status of wills of head/heads of the family

   b. Proposed new will

      i. Choice of executor

      ii. Jurisdiction where wills laws will apply

      iii. Funeral arrangements

      iv. Likely debts

      v. Special debts

         - income tax

         - probate fees

      vi. Trusts for children/grandchildren (if applicable)

      vii. Special financial needs considerations

         - Disabled dependants

         - unemployed dependants etc.

      viii. Specific gifts to friends and family

      ix. Charitable gifts

      x. Division of residue

xi. Financial treatment of surviving spouse

xii. Dealing with specific items

- family cottage
- family business
- privately held shares in a corporation
- other

xiii. Family law claims

- financial inclusion and/or exclusion of in-laws
- guardianship of minor children
- current status of powers of attorney
- proposed new powers of attorney and discussions regarding choice of attorney both for personal care and for finances
- wind-up steps including signing the family constitution

5. Proposed power of attorney for property and personal care

6. Create and sign the family constitution

While the agenda is obviously a key component for a successful conference, the meeting process itself can be just as critical. If the conference begins with the head of the family describing his or her estate plan in an autocratic manner that discourages discussion, the family members are less likely to buy in to both the idea of the meeting and the estate plan itself.

You want to encourage your family members to take a meaningful role in the decision-making process so that they feel that they have participated in your estate plan rather than have it be imposed on them. As a parent, it may be difficult for you to hand over some decision-making power to your children, but it is important that you do so if you want the meeting to be a success and your children to feel bound by its results.

In order for the conference to succeed, all members of the family need to participate. Here are three suggestions that can help:

1. **The time set aside for the conference should be flexible**. A family conference can consist of more than one meeting. Although the initial meeting of the conference is usually fairly lengthy, subsequent meetings can be very brief. The length of and need for subsequent meetings will depend on the specific circumstances of your family members. For example, if one child has to travel a great distance to attend, he or she will likely prefer to cover as much as possible in one meeting, rather than having to return again to continue the conference at a subsequent meeting. On the other hand, if you have family members who are in ill health or elderly, they may be unable to sit through a long meeting. You will have to weigh the needs of your family members and decide what is appropriate in your situation.
2. **Leave room for agenda flexibility.** While the chairperson will decide whether items can be added to the meeting agenda, it should be made clear to family members that any issues not addressed at a particular meeting will be put on the agenda for a subsequent meeting. Family members will not feel part of the decision-making process if the family conference has not addressed the issues that are important to them.
3. **If any family decision is made that affects the whole family, it requires unanimous consent**. The family conference is intended to achieve consensus, not majority rule. You need to obtain unanimous consent on all decisions affecting the whole family. If one family member objects to a decision, you need to address his or her concerns. While this may appear onerous, keep in mind

that it only takes one dissatisfied beneficiary to start estate litigation — which is exactly what you are trying to prevent.

Your commitment to this process will set the tone for the conference. However, the presence of a professional mediator encourages this process because it tells the family members that the conference is different from a normal family get-together and that different rules apply. Family members will then display a greater willingness to listen to each other's positions and consider viewpoints that are different from those which they might ordinarily demonstrate.

CHOICE OF CHAIRPERSON

In general, you (or possibly your spouse) should act as the chairperson for the first meeting of the family conference. Acting as the initial chairperson allows you to set the tone for the meeting and to ensure that the discussion remains on topic. In addition, in most cases family members are more comfortable recognizing and deferring to the authority of the head of the family than to another family member, such as a sibling.

The mediator will also play a significant role in ensuring the smooth running of the meeting. The mediator will have gone through the family conference process many times, while family members, including the chairperson, will be new to the process. Not surprisingly, family members often look to the mediator as a *de facto* chairperson at certain points in a meeting, especially when unresolved issues emerge and a neutral third party is best able to steer the meeting in a productive direction.

CHAPTER 16

AT THE CONFERENCE

As the sample agenda in the previous Chapter sets out, most family conferences will start with the mediator, who will explain his or her role to the family members and highlight the rules governing the meeting.

After that, the meeting will follow the agenda you have prepared. At the end of the meeting and depending on its success, your family should either approve and sign the family constitution or develop an action plan to address outstanding issues and schedule a further meeting.

ROLE OF THE MEDIATOR

It is essential that the mediator remain neutral throughout the family conference process. This means that he or she cannot provide any legal advice to anyone in the family, including the person making the will. For this reason, it is inappropriate for your lawyer to act as the mediator of the meeting. However, since your lawyer will be heavily involved in developing and implementing your estate plan, it will be very helpful for him or her to attend the family conference to provide information and assistance.

The family members should be told that the mediator has not been involved in the preparation of the estate plan. When I am acting as mediator, I find that once the family members understand that I have not prepared the estate plan, they treat me as a valuable resource for solving problems that may arise, rather than the source of the problems themselves.

When I act as mediator, I ask family members to sign two agreements at the start of the meeting:

- the family conference agreement
- the rules for the family conference

A family conference agreement sets the stage for the meeting and emphasizes my neutral role as mediator and the confidential nature of the meeting itself. The rules for the family conference outline the type of conduct that is expected from all participants.

FAMILY CONFERENCE AGREEMENT

Noted below is a sample of a family conference agreement that I use:

Family Conference Agreement of the Gordon Family

[LIST NAMES OF ALL PARTICIPANTS]

AND IN THE MATTER OF THE FAMILY CONFERENCE PROCESS WITH THE ABOVE-NAMED PARTIES BEFORE IAN M. HULL OF HULL & HULL ("the Mediator"), with respect to the family matters arising in the above noted family.

The parties have entered into this Family Conference Agreement with the Mediator with the intention of reaching a consensual settlement of their family's estate plan.

The provisions of this Agreement are as follows:

1. The Mediator is a neutral mediator who will help the participants prepare their own written family constitution. The Mediator will not provide an assessment of the merits of the family plan unless requested to do so by all parties, and only if the Mediator deems it advisable to do so.

2. The Mediator does not offer legal advice, nor does he or she provide legal counsel. Each party may retain his/her/its own lawyer in order to be properly counselled about his/her/its legal interests, rights and obligations.

3. It is understood that in order for the family conference to work, open and honest communications are essential. Accordingly, all written and oral communications, negotiations and statements made in the course of the family conference process will be treated as privileged settlement discussions and are absolutely confidential and without prejudice. Therefore:

    a) The parties and any person attending the family conference with any party agree that all communications and documents shared which are not otherwise discoverable shall be without prejudice and shall be kept confidential as against the outside world, and shall not be used, in discovery, cross-examination, at trial or in any other way, in this or any other proceeding.

b) The parties agree that they will not at any time, before, during, or after the family conference process, call the Mediator or anyone associated with Hull & Hull as witnesses in any legal or administrative proceedings concerning issues raised in the family conference. To the extent that they may have a right to call the Mediator or anyone associated with Hull & Hull as witnesses, that right is hereby waived.

c) The parties agree not to subpoena or seek any court order or use any other legal process in an attempt to demand the production of any records, notes, work, product or the like of the Mediator in any legal or administrative proceedings concerning issues raised in the family conference. To the extent that they may have the right to demand these documents, that right is hereby waived.

d) The Mediator shall not be liable for anything done or omitted with respect to the family conference process and has the immunity granted to a judge under the *Courts of Justice Act of Ontario* and or any other applicable law.

The effect of this agreement is to treat the family conference like true mediation, in that the mediator cannot be subpoenaed or required to give evidence about the family conference. It also means that information and documents shared at the family conference that are privileged (meaning they would not be required to be disclosed in a litigation proceeding) will maintain their privileged status if litigation occurs. This is to encourage the full disclosure of information at the family conference without the family members worrying about whether their disclosure could subsequently be used against them.

RULES FOR THE MEETING

The mediator should also review the rules for the meeting with the family members. The rules are designed to promote an atmosphere of mutual respect and courtesy. Each of the family members should be asked to sign a copy of the rules at the start of the meeting to emphasize their importance.

Here is a set of rules that I use at family conferences:

Rules for the Gordon Family Conference

1. With a view to working toward family harmony during their lifetimes and after their deaths, David and Barbara Gordon are committed to full and frank disclosure of their estate planning intentions through the family conference process. All participants will enter into the family conference process in an honest and forthright manner.

2. David and Barbara Gordon will govern the family conference process, assisted by mediator Ian Hull.

3. The participants acknowledge and understand that while the mediator Ian Hull is a neutral party, he is being paid by David and Barbara Gordon.

4. All of the participants agree and acknowledge that the information exchanged throughout the family conference process, whether orally or in writing, shall remain confidential and not be disclosed outside the family, except as otherwise provided in the Family Conference Agreement of the Gordon Family (hereinafter referred to as the "Gordon Family Conference Agreement".

5. All the participants shall use a professional and businesslike approach throughout the discussions and shall refrain from any harsh language, whether direct or indirect.

6. The participants agree to be bound by the terms of the Gordon Family Conference Agreement and will confirm their agreement by signing a copy of the Family Conference Agreement prior to the beginning of the initial family conference session.

7. It is understood that any one or all of the participants may leave the family conference at any time and that notwithstanding their departure, they will continue to be bound by the terms of the Gordon Family Conference Agreement, in-

cluding the terms with respect to the privacy and confidentiality of information exchanged at the conference.

These rules can, of course, be amended to reflect the needs of each individual family. In some situations, family members attending the meeting may propose additional rules or amendments to the rules you have suggested. You will then have to decide whether those changes are acceptable to you, and if so, incorporate them into the meeting rules.

NEED FOR FULL DISCLOSURE

There is one rule for the family conference that applies primarily to you and your spouse: you need to fully disclose the details of your estate plan to your family members. While this can be extremely difficult, full disclosure is essential to the success of the family conference process. If you fail to provide full disclosure, you will create an atmosphere of mistrust that will poison the process.

More important, your goal in holding a family conference is to obtain your family members' approval of your estate plan so that they will not challenge it. If, after your death, they discover that you did not fully disclose the details of your estate plan, their feelings of betrayal will increase the likelihood that they will challenge your will.

In some cases, it may be harder to openly discuss emotional issues than financial issues, particularly in families that are reticent about airing their feelings. However, it is far preferable for your children to know, and understand, your true feelings while you are alive than to be informed of them after your death when they may misinterpret your intentions.

Tackling Tough Issues at a Family Conference

Sam and Julie Verma have two children, both in their thirties. Their daughter Amy is a successful fashion designer. Their son Jacob has struggled with alcohol and drug problems since he was in university. While he periodically enters treatment centres, he is unable to remain sober for any length of time.

Past family discussions about Jacob's drug and alcohol use inevitably became extremely heated and often ended with Jacob refusing to speak to his parents for an extended period of time, so Sam and Julie now completely avoid the subject in order to preserve peace in the family.

> Sam and Julie decide to divide their estate into two shares. They are leaving Amy one share outright, and using the other share to set up a trust for Jacob. The trust will ensure that Jacob's living expenses are paid, but will not give him direct access to large sums of money that he might spend on drugs or alcohol.
>
> Sam and Julie dread holding a family conference because of their reluctance to discuss Jacob's addiction problems, but they proceed with the exercise. Julie prepares what she wants to say in advance. She tells both children how much she loves them, and tells Jacob how worried she and Sam are about him and his future. She explains that they have structured their estate so that they will know that his needs will be taken care of, in the best way they know how. Because of his mother's words, Jacob realizes that his parents have set up a trust for him because they care about him, not because they prefer his sister, and recognizes the benefits of the trust in securing his long-term future.
>
> Consider the alternative: at the family conference, Sam and Julie tell their children that they will each receive half of the estate, but they do not explain that Amy will receive her share outright while Jacob's share will be held in trust. When they die and their actual plans are revealed, Jacob feels furious and betrayed: his parents said they would each receive the same share, and now his sister has a large sum of money to her name and he has a monthly allowance. He decides to challenge the will.

There are a number of subjects that you may find particularly difficult to discuss with your family members. Most people do not like talking about estate planning, because it requires them to contemplate either their own death or the death of a loved one. That natural reluctance may be compounded if there are additional topics you would rather not discuss with your children. These topics may include:

- **Extramarital relationships**. No one wants his or her children to know if they had an extramarital relationship, especially if there are children from that relationship, but if it affects your estate plan you need to let your family members know.
- **Unequal treatment of children**. It can be very difficult to explain to your children why you are treating them differently. It is important to remember that your goal is fairness, and that fair and equal are not always the same.

- **Spendthrift beneficiaries**. You may have beneficiaries who are not financially responsible or who have addiction or gambling problems and who are likely to misuse any funds you leave them. You can create "spendthrift trusts" to provide them with income, but not capital. If you are creating spendthrift trusts, you need to tell those beneficiaries, and your other family members, at the family conference.
- **Family law concerns**. You may dislike your child's spouse, or be concerned that his or her marriage is unlikely to last. If so, your lawyer should ensure that the value of any property you leave your child is not considered to be part of his or her net family property if the marriage ends, and that the spouse cannot make a claim against the specific property you leave your child. This is especially important if you are leaving your children shares of a private company. Again, you will have to discuss your concerns with family members.
- **Special needs beneficiaries**. You may have special needs beneficiaries who will need to be looked after for the rest of their lives. You can establish special trusts in your will to provide for them. Because they will require permanent support, you may have to leave a greater share of your estate to the trust than to your other beneficiaries, who may be disappointed in how you are dividing your estate.
- **Family business issues**. If more than one of your children are involved in your family business, you will have to determine which one should succeed you and create a business succession plan as part of your estate plan. You may find that communicating your choice of successor to your family members, particularly the family members you do not choose, is extremely difficult.
- **Incentive trusts**. If your children are expecting to receive a large inheritance when you die, they may be unpleasantly surprised to learn you have established an incentive trust instead. In addition, they may not agree with your choice of the behaviour the trust is to reward.

If one of the topics you need to address at the family conference is particularly sensitive, give careful thought in advance as to what you want to say. Your mediator can help you decide the best way to raise the topic with your family. If the topic is particularly upsetting (such as an out-of-wedlock child), your family may need some time to get used to it before they are able to proceed with the estate plan. Your family conference should be structured accordingly.

COURSE OF THE CONFERENCE

The family conference itself should follow the agenda that you prepared in advance. When I act as mediator, I begin the meeting by introducing myself and describing the process that will be used and the goals for the meeting. I then give an outline of the proposed estate plan. I call this the "view from 30,000 feet" because it is a broad overview of the estate plan that describes the key dispositions that will occur without going into detail.

You, and possibly your spouse, will then follow with your opening statements, which are usually quite short and often reiterate the goals and thank family members for participating.

Your lawyer then will provide a detailed explanation of your estate plan, and answer any questions raised by family members. Once the family members understand the details of your proposed estate plan, they should split into smaller groups or caucuses, where their concerns can be openly discussed. Based on what the mediator has observed in the meeting, he or she will usually suggest how the caucus groups will be split, in order to achieve maximum effectiveness.

When I act as mediator, I often like to separate the children during the caucus sessions. This allows the children to raise issues that they might be uncomfortable raising in a larger group. This is especially important if the estate is being divided unequally, but can also be useful even when the estate is being divided equally.

For example, if you have two children, it would seem to be fair to divide your estate equally between them. However, if one child lives in another country, and the other lives nearby and has spent a great deal of time taking care of you, it may not be fair at all in that child's eyes. Dividing the children into separate caucuses will allow your children to raise those concerns openly without worrying about seeming ungrateful or creating problems.

As the mediator, I move between the caucuses and the parents. Initially, my focus is not on resolving any issues that are raised at the caucuses but in ensuring that they are identified so they can be addressed later. In many cases, the concerns raised in the caucuses are set aside while the family reunites in a joint session to discuss the rest of the estate plan.

As the conference goes on, it will become clear which issues are dividing the family. The mediator promotes negotiation on these issues and suggests possible ways of resolving them. In some cases, an agreement will be reached at the first meeting. In other cases, the family members may need time to consider their positions and consider the possible courses of action. This is especially true for the parents if it becomes clear that the estate plan needs substantial amendment. In that case, the conference may need to be adjourned while the estate plan is amended and then reconvened when the new proposal is completed.

The goal of the family conference is to sign a family constitution that approves the estate plan. If the first meeting goes well, that may happen in one day. If all the family members have not approved the estate plan at the end of the first meeting, the mediator should summarize the points of agreement that have been reached and the items that are outstanding. An ongoing record should be made of the agreements that have been reached and an action plan developed to address outstanding issues. The action plan should clearly identify what needs to be done and who is responsible for doing it. Once the task is completed, a record of its completion can be created at a subsequent meeting.

Before the first meeting is adjourned, the family members should set a date for the next meeting, and agree on what will be discussed at that meeting. This process can continue until the estate plan is approved and a family constitution signed.

Whether or not a family constitution is approved, a journal and ongoing record of all meetings of the family conference should be kept. This allows family members to easily review the progress that has been made and identify any issues that remain outstanding.

CHAPTER 17

IF FAMILY MEMBERS WILL NOT APPROVE YOUR PLAN

In some situations, and despite your best efforts, one or more family member may not approve your estate plan. Sometimes family members will not even attend the family conference where the estate plan is being discussed. It may be worth letting some time pass, and then trying the process again. Unfortunately, you cannot postpone finalizing your estate plan indefinitely, so you may have to go ahead without the participation of all of your family members.

IF FAMILY MEMBERS WILL NOT ATTEND THE FAMILY CONFERENCE

If some of your family members will not attend the family conference, you can still use the family conference process to obtain the agreement of your other family members. Once a family constitution is signed, the mediator can send it to the non-participating family members and invite them to sign it. This may spark their interest in the process and they may be willing to become subsequently involved.

Hold the family conference anyway

Marion Barker, a widow, wants to hold a family conference with her four children to discuss how she will dispose of her family home, which is her only significant asset. She has previously told her four children that she intends to leave the house to her son James, who has looked after her for the last ten years.

Two of Marion's children were extremely upset when Marion told them of her plans for the home and refused to attend the meeting, despite Marion's invitations and the mediator's efforts. The family conference goes ahead, attended by Marion, James, James' new wife Suzanne and James' sister Lisa.

> Although Lisa does not object to James receiving the home, at the family conference she realizes that if James were to die shortly after Marion, Suzanne would receive the home and not her. Lisa wants the home to stay in the family. Although James is initially reluctant to commit to how he will leave the home in his will, he understands his sister's concerns. The family members sign a family constitution in which James agrees to pass on any remaining assets to his siblings on his death.
>
> Marion, Lisa, James and Suzanne sign a family constitution, which also refers to the fact that Marion has appointed Lisa as her attorney under her power of attorney. The mediator sends the family constitution, along with copies of Marion's will and power of attorney, to the other two children and asks them to sign it. One of the children signs but the other refuses to do so.

Even if the non-participating family members will not sign the family constitution, it is likely that a court will consider the process favourably if the will or power of attorney is subsequently challenged. First, it will be difficult for unhappy family members to argue that you lacked testamentary capacity or were unduly influenced, because your lawyer would typically have attended the family conference and would have comprehensive notes about what occurred. Second, circulating the family constitution, even to the non-participating family members, shows your clear and sincere intention as to how you want your assets divided.

IF FAMILY MEMBERS OBJECT TO YOUR PROPOSED ESTATE PLAN

In some cases, family members may attend the family conference, but refuse to approve your proposed estate plan. If that occurs, you may want to amend your estate plan to satisfy as many of the concerns of your unhappy family members as possible — without sacrificing your personal goals. Again, make sure they receive a copy of the family constitution even if they will not sign it.

If you still think there is a good chance that a family member may challenge your estate after you have passed away, make sure your lawyer has included *in terrorem* clauses in your will that provide that anyone challenging the will forfeits all gifts made to him or her under the will.

You should also prepare detailed notes about your family member's concerns and the steps you have taken to satisfy them. They may be useful in protecting your estate from a successful challenge. Unfortunately, they will not prevent the disgruntled family member from launching that challenge.

Chapter 18

Steps to Take After the Conference

Once the family conference is finished, you will still have work to do in order for your estate plan to take effect. If the family conference has been a success, your lawyer can begin drafting the documents necessary to implement the estate plan. If the family conference has not been successful, you will have to consider what course of action to take.

IMPLEMENTING YOUR ESTATE PLAN

Once a family constitution is signed, your lawyer and your other professional advisors will prepare the documents necessary to implement your estate plan, including wills, trusts, powers of attorney and deeds of gift. You may find that minor issues arise during the course of the implementation process that you had not anticipated. Depending on the nature of those issues, you can choose to either resolve the issue yourself or hold a brief supplementary meeting with your family members.

> **Small Changes Still Need Family Agreement**
>
> Following a family conference, Oren Taylor divided his estate between his three adult children and a trust for his grandchildren. After the conference, he realizes that he does not want the grandchildren to have the right to the capital of the trust when they turn 18 years old, but he did not raise that issue at the meeting. He holds a brief conference call with his three children and they all agree that the grandchildren will need to be 25 years old before they have the right to the capital.

REVIEW YOUR ESTATE PLAN REGULARLY

Once your estate plan is finalized and all the necessary documents have been prepared, you will likely experience both relief and satisfaction in knowing that the process is over. However, you need to be diligent in reviewing your estate plan regularly to ensure it still reflects your wishes. In Chapter 12, we discussed changes in your personal circumstances that should cause you to review your estate plan. You should review it immediately if any such changes occur. Even if there are no major changes in your personal circumstances, you should still review your plan every few years.

If you make changes to your estate plan, you will have to consider whether you need another family conference. In some cases, you may decide that a meeting is not necessary because the changes are not substantial. However, you should err on the side of caution if you are not sure. It is preferable to hold a brief meeting that may be unnecessary than to create feelings of mistrust in your family members about the family conference process and your commitment to full disclosure.

At the time of the initial conference, you may want to discuss the possibility that your estate plan will be amended and commit to holding further conferences when that occurs. You may also be able to identify situations where further conferences may not be necessary or when, instead of a conference meeting, a telephone conference may be more appropriate. For example, if you own a corporation that undergoes a reorganization, you may make changes to the estate plan that do not affect the division of ownership on your death. In such a case, a family conference is not required before making the change.

CHAPTER 19

CONCLUSION

There are simply no substitutes for effective communication in the estate planning process. A carefully thought out estate plan is one half of the process. The other half is disclosing all of its details to your family members and working through their areas of concern. It does not matter how much money you spend on the first half; if you neglect the second half you risk sacrificing all of your careful planning and expert advice — and a substantial portion of your assets.

As a litigation lawyer, I continue to be shocked at what families are capable of doing to each other after the death of a loved one. Even the closest families can be permanently torn apart by an estate dispute. Yet most of these fights are completely preventable — so long as there is open communication and frank discussion about the estate plan before it is too late.

Since it is impossible to accurately predict the source of family problems after the death of a loved one, families who talk to each other openly about the details of their estate plan, before their deaths can protect themselves from those problems. The family head reaps the financial and emotional benefits of knowing that their loved ones are satisfied with the arrangements they have made and are unlikely to contest their estate.

While there is no way to entirely predict the success each family will achieve in working through the estate plan together with a professional mediator, based on my experience, it is the best way to prevent estate litigation and protect your estate.

INDEX

A

Accounting duties
- described, 26
- formal accounts, 27
- informal accounts, 27
- types of, 26

Assets
- executor's duty re. *See* **Executor**
- investment of, 27
- mix and nature of, 58

B

Breach of contract, 61

C

Capital gains taxes, 30-31, 34-35
Codicil, 14
Constructive trust claim, 61
Costs of estate litigation
- generally, 63-64
- mediation, 66-67
- stages in court action
- • appeal, 66
- • collecting and disclosing evidence, 64
- • discoveries, 65
- • order organizing litigation, 64
- • pre-trial conference, 65
- • trial, 65-66

Court action. *See* **Costs of estate litigation**

D

Debts, 20
Dependants' relief claims, 59-60

E

Estate freeze
- control issues, 44
- example of, 43-44
- family trust, use of, 45
- purpose of, 43

Estate litigation, *see also* **Will**
- causes of, 55-58
- • acrimonious **extended family**, 56
- • actions of personal representatives, 58
- • frailties and secrets, 57
- • inadequate estate planning advice, 56
- • ignorance of need for estate plan, 55
- • intransigent family members, 57
- • mix and nature of assets, 58
- • out of date estate plan, 55
- • poorly drafted documents, 57
- • reluctance to seek advice, 56
- costs of. *See* **Costs of estate litigation**
- will, claims against, 58-61
- • breach of contract, 61
- • constructive trust claim, 61
- • dependants' relief claims, 59-60
- • *Family Law Act* claims, 60
- • *quantum meruit* claim, 61

Estate plan, *see also* **Family conference**
- challenging. *See* **Estate litigation**
- changes to, agreement re, 97
- conflicts, minimizing, 1-2
- estate protection strategies, 1-2
- implementation of, 97
- objections to, 94-95
- purposes of
- • allocation of assets, 7
- • disability, protection of assets in event of, 7
- • estate tax bill, reduction of, 7
- regular review of, 98

Executor
- accounting duties. *See* **Accounting duties**
- assets
- • collection and distribution by, 20-22
- • • estate litigation and, 20
- • investment of, 27
- choice of, factors, 19
- debts, payment of, 20
- distributions, timing of, 21
- duties of
- • asset collection and distribution, 20-22
- • final tax return, filing, 22
- • funeral arrangements, making, 22
- • information to beneficiaries, providing, 22
- • locating will, 22
- fees, 23-24
- generally, 10, 19
- income tax duties. *See* **Income tax filings**
- powers and authority of, 22
- probate, application for, 21
- professionals, use of by, 24
- removal of, 24
- role of, 19-24

F

Family conference, *see also* **Family constitution**
- agenda
- • example of, 77-79
- • preparation of, 77

Family conference — *cont'd*
- agreement, example, 84-85
- chair, choice of, 81
- course of, 90-91
- full disclosure, need for, 87-90
  - extramarital relationships, 88
  - family business issues, 89
  - family law concerns, 89
  - incentive trust, 89
  - special needs beneficiaries, 89
  - spendthrift beneficiaries, 89
  - tough issues, tackling, 87-89
  - unequal treatment of children, 88
- generally, 2
- invitees, 75-76
- refusal to attend, 93-94
- location of, 76
- mediator, role of, 83-86, 90-91
- meeting, rules for, 85-87
- minor children, 76-77
- objections to estate plan, 94-95
  - *in terrorem* clauses, 94-95
- participation
  - non-participants, 93-94
  - strategies to encourage, 80-81
- post-conference steps, 97-98
- preliminary considerations, 75-81
- purposes of, 2

Family constitution
- example of, 71-72
- generally, 71
- wording of, 71-73

***Family Law Act* claims**, 60
Family trust, 38, 45
Fees, executor's, 23-24

I

Incentive trust, 38, 41-42, 89
Income tax, *see also* **Taxes arising on death**
- capital gains, 30-31, 34-35
- filings. *See* **Income tax filings**
- final return, 22

Income tax filings
- clearance certificate, application for, 26
- previously unfiled returns, 25
- T1 terminal return, 25
- T3 estate return, 25
- T3 final distribution return, 26

Intestacy
- consequences of, 11
- minors, 11
- statutory division of property, 11

Investment of estate assets, 27

L

Litigation
- costs of. *See* **Costs of estate litigation**

Litigation — *cont'd*
- estate. *See* **Estate litigation**

M

Mediation, 66-67, 83-86, 90-91
Minors, 11, 66-67

P

Power of attorney
- described, 47
- for personal care, 52
- for property, 47-51
  - challenges to, 51
  - choice of attorney, 49-50
  - joint attorney, 49
  - limited purpose, 47
  - mental capacity requirement, 48
  - neutral party as attorney, 50
  - restrictions on authority of attorney, 48-49

Probate, 21, 34-35

Q

***Quantum meruit* claim**, 61

R

Real estate. *See* **Recreational property**
Recreational property
- capital gains taxes, plan for, 30-31
- conflict over, 29-30
- generally, 29-30

RRSP/RRIF, 34

S

Special needs beneficiary trust, 38, 89
Spendthrift trust, 37, 89
Spousal trust, 38

T

Taxes arising on death, *see also* **Income tax**
- capital gains taxes, 34-35
  - principal residence exemption, 34
- generally, 34
- probate fees, reduction of, 34-5
- RRSP and RRIF assets, 34
- tax reduction strategies, 35

Trusts
- advantages of, 38-39
- described, 37-38
- incentive trust, 38, 41-2
- trustee
  - choice of, factors re, 39-40
- types of, 37-8
  - family trust, 38, 45
  - incentive trust, 38

Trusts — *cont'd*
- • income trust, 37
- • special needs beneficiary trust, 38
- • spendthrift trust, 37
- • spousal trust, 38

U

Undue influence claim, 14

W

Will, *see also* **Intestacy**
- addition to, 14
- amendments to, 12
- challenge of. *See* contesting
- codicil, 14
- contesting, *see also* **Estate litigation, will, claims against**
- • by beneficiary, 16
- • contract not to contest, 16

Will, see also Intestacy — *cont'd*
- • *in terrorem* clause, 16
- described, 9
- execution of
- • mental capacity requirement, 13
- • signature requirements, 14
- executor of, 10
- formal, 12
- holograph will, 12
- letters, 17
- locating, 22
- minors, 11
- property division provisions, 9
- residue, division of, 10
- specific bequests, 10
- trust provisions, 10
- types of, 12
- undue influence claim, 14
- witnesses, 14

Will-like dispositions, 17